DATE DUE

film music

screencraft

mark russell
& james young

film music

screencraft

series devised by barbara mercer

Focal Press

Boston Oxford Auckland Johannesburg Melbourne New Delhi

Focal Press is an imprint of

Butterworth-Heinemann

A member of the Reed-Elsevier Group

http://www.focalpress.com

The publisher offers special discounts on
bulk orders of this book. For information,
please contact:
Manager of Special Sales
Butterworth-Heinemann
225 Wildwood Avenue
Woburn, MA 01801-2041
Tel: 781-904-2500
Fax: 781-904-2620

ISBN 0-240-80441-4

10 9 8 7 6 5 4 3 2 1

Design Copyright © 1998 Morla Design, Inc., San Francisco

Layout by Artmedia, London

Production and separation by ProVision Pte. Ltd., Singapore

Tel: +65 334 7720

Fax: +65 334 7721

"SILENCE OF THE LAMBS"
28-6   (50)

8M3   "THE BEATING"   COMP. H. SHORE
ORCH. H. DENISON

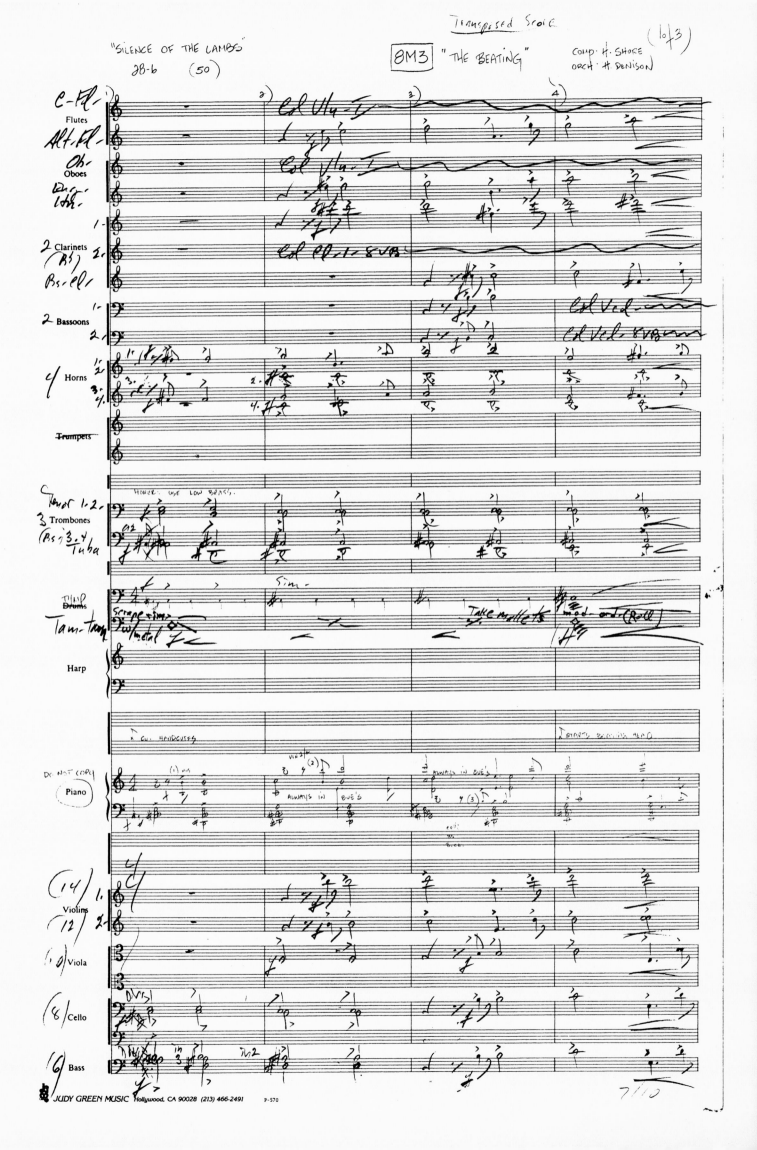

contents

introduction

"Cinema is undoubtably the most important artistic development of the 20th century." So said Bernard Herrmann, the single most influential dramatic film composer of the century. Cinema, and more recently television, have certainly become the greatest patrons of commissioned music of our time. In the 18th century Mozart and Haydn wrote dinner music for their employers and Bach dashed off a Church Cantata every week. Today, countless composers, orchestras, conductors, orchestrators, copyists, music editors, music contractors, music supervisors, studios, music engineers, and agents are kept busy by the film and television industry.

And the modern film composer is now a recording star as well. It's not unusual for a soundtrack album to sell over one million copies, in fact some sell many more (**Titanic** (1997) to date has sold eleven million and **The Lion King** (1994) ten million). Composers like John Barry, Michael Nyman, John Williams and James Horner all have their own recording contracts, not just for film music but for new concert works. Film composers have their own internet sites, often run by enthusiasts and you can follow their every move in magazines like *Film Score Monthly*. With declining interest and falling sales in contemporary classical music, record companies are looking to film composers to provide today's accessible, popular orchestral music.

The power of the music score is easy to evaluate. Just try watching **Planet of the Apes** (1968) or **Psycho** (1960) with the sound turned down and it's immediately obvious that Jerry Goldsmith's and Bernard Herrmann's ingenious, chilling scores carry almost all of the tension and drama. When Hitchcock first saw the rushes for **Psycho** he was so disappointed that he decided to turn it into a one-hour television drama. Fortunately, Bernard Herrmann convinced him that he could change the mood of the film with his music, and the result is one of the most memorable scores of all time.

L'Arrivée d'un train à la Ciotat (1895, Lumière brothers)

The Battleship Potemkin (1925, Sergei Eisenstein)

October (1927, Sergei Eisenstein)

Napoléon (1927, Abel Gance)

But how did music come to be so central in its association with film? Today the score is often used to convey what the word cannot, a musical version of the Greek chorus, but in the early days of silent films the music accompaniment told the whole story. From the first flickering images of trains and workhouses conjured up by the Lumière brothers at the turn of the century there was a piano performing a medley of appropriate classical themes and popular tunes, doing its best to keep up with the picture. For action scenes Rossini's 'William Tell Overture' was hastily wheeled out, whereas no romantic scene would be complete without Tchaikovsky's 'Pathetique Symphony' or Isolde's lovesong from Wagner's 'Tristan and Isolde'. But the honour of having written the first actual film score goes to the celebrated French composer Camille Saint-Saëns. In 1908 he composed music for the filmed theatre production of 'L'Assassinat du Duc de Guise'. He later developed this music into a concert piece, his 'Opus 128' for strings, piano and harmonium, but, mainly due to the expense, the idea of specially composed scores did not catch on. Instead manuscript books with suggestions of music to fit specific moods or dramatic situations became the norm for theatre orchestras and pianists everywhere.

When silent film turned into talking pictures Hollywood studio heads brought over Europe's most respected composers; they became advisors and orchestrators who could edit classical music to fit scenes. But it wasn't until Max Steiner, the Viennese godson of Richard Strauss, convinced producer David O. Selznick to let him compose some original cues for **Symphony of Six Million** (1932) that the full significance of a specially composed dramatic underscore was grasped. Such was the effect of those few scenes on audiences that, soon, every Hollywood studio had to have its own music department with its roster of composers. The following year Steiner composed the seminal score which was responsible for shaping the classic Hollywood sound. In **King Kong** (1933) he borrowed from opera the concept of leitmotifs, devices where a character or situation has its own recurring melody or texture and embedded them in the opulent orchestral textures of late 19th-century romanticism. His through-composed score, for the first time fully integrated with the picture, set the template for film music which still exists today. When you listen to John Williams' soundtracks for the **Star Wars** trilogy and his more recent **The Lost World: Jurassic Park** (1997) (a deliberate homage to Steiner's **King Kong**) it's obvious that, in mainstream movies, apart from the introduction of a few modernisms, nothing much has changed in the art of film scoring. Steiner went on to refine his technique in **Gone With the Wind** (1939), a year when, incredibly, he wrote a total of eleven film scores.

But in Russia something altogether different was going on. Director Sergei Eisenstein's silent epics **The Battleship Potemkin** (1925) and **October** (1927) demanded a different kind of score. **The Battleship Potemkin** dealt with the historic mutiny aboard a battleship during the unsuccessful revolution of 1905. Eisenstein said of the music "the audience must be lashed into a fury and shaken violently by the sound... this sound can't be strong enough and should be tuned to the limit of the audience's physical and mental

Symphony of Six Million (1932, Gregory La Cava)

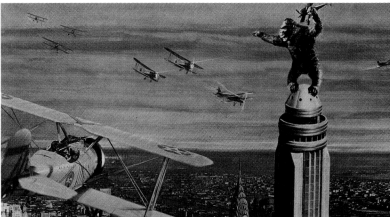
King Kong (1933, Merian C. Cooper)

Alexander Nevsky (1938, Sergei Eisenstein)

High Noon (1952, Fred Zinnemann)

Gone With the Wind (1939, David O. Selznick)

capacity." The German composer Edmund Meisel took him at his word, and aided by a colossal battery of percussion, created an orchestral score of immense dramatic power, which radically increased the punch of the film. In fact, so overwhelming was Meisel's score that on the film's release in Germany it was banned. But this ground-breaking soundtrack showed that accompanying music didn't merely have to mimic the screen action, but could create a much more complex set of relationships with the movie – and it could be expressed in a contemporary musical language. This tradition of scoring silent classics continues today with Carl Davis' monumental reworkings of **Intolerance** (1916) and **Napoléon** (1927) and, in a rather more modernistic vein, with Philip Glass' minimalist soundtracks for films like **Dracula** (1931) and **La Belle et la Bête** (1946). Eisenstein later forged a similarly fruitful association with the famed Russian composer Sergei Prokofiev for the nationalistic epic **Alexander Nevsky** (1938). Theirs was a truly two-way collaboration; in some

places the director cut scenes to fit pre-recorded music, in others the composer wrote to the final cut – a method and relationship later mirrored by Peter Greenaway's partnership with composer Michael Nyman and Godfrey Reggio's with Philip Glass, both in the 1980s – but a way of working that was unthinkable at that time in Hollywood.

Back in America, however, this was soon to change with the collaboration between Orson Welles and Bernard Herrmann on **Citizen Kane** (1941). Herrmann was involved from the very outset of production. He was present on set and constantly made notes; his score was recorded over a long period of time and dubbed on to the film in sections. Herrmann said of the film "**Citizen Kane** was so unusual, technically, that it afforded me many unique opportunities for musical experiment. It abounded in montages, which were long enough to permit me to compose complete musical numbers, rather than mere cues to fit them. The emotional

Psycho (1960, Alfred Hitchcock)

impact of these musical numbers was much greater than that of background music, which has no beginning or ending." In fact, in an echo of Eisenstein and Prokofiev, Welles cut his film to fit these complete musical pieces. Herrmann redefined the dramatic potential of music to picture in this and in his collaborations with Alfred Hitchcock. In the process he updated Hollywood's musical language, making modernistic orchestrations and harmonies widely accepted, and in his use of repetitive rhythmic cells he predated minimalism by some twenty years.

Film subjects tended to come in cycles. In the early and mid-1940s a popular one was the psychological thriller, usually involving a main character with a psychological defect, like amnesia. One of the better movies of this type was Hitchcock's **Spellbound** (1945) with an Oscar-winning score by the Hungarian-born Miklos Rosza. To heighten the sense of eeriness and to describe the hero's warped mental state

Rosza used an electronic instrument, the "theremin". This is an instrument played by hand movements controlling sound-wave oscillations; it has a vast range and produces a ghostly sound almost as expressive as the human voice. Of course, once Rosza got the idea past producer David O. Selznick, Hollywood loved it, and the theremin became flavour of the month. But it had opened the door to electronics and alternative sounds, especially in science fiction and horror movies. The apotheosis of this in a mainstream movie was the first totally electronic score by Louis and Bebe Barron for **Forbidden Planet** (1956). In fact their music was so extreme that it was described as "electronic tonalities". They invented their own electronic circuit boards for each character, so raising Max Steiner's concept of distinct leitmotifs to a new level. It's a score that still sounds fresh and exciting and is a good example of film music developing in parallel with concert music. German composer Stockhausen was working along similar electro-acoustic lines at the time.

East of Eden (1955, Elia Kazan)

Forbidden Planet (1956, Fred M. Wilcox)

The Graduate (1967, Mike Nichols)

Star Wars (1977, George Lucas)

In fact this relationship with concert music is an important one; film has a worldwide audience and through this movie goers have unwittingly become accustomed to the development of 20th-century classical music. Through Leonard Rosenman's avant-garde scores for **East of Eden** (1955) and **The Cobweb** (1955) many people would have heard serial music for the first time. Through the soundtrack for **2001: A Space Odyssey** (1968) the atmospheric works of Hungarian composer György Ligeti would have become familiar. Now it is totally acceptable for a mainstream score to encompass a modernistic soundworld; John Williams' exhilarating atonal music for **Close Encounters of the Third Kind** (1977) and parts of Ennio Morricone's ground-breaking score for **The Mission** (1986) are obvious examples.

While Rosenman was bringing cutting-edge orchestral modernism to Hollywood, Elmer Bernstein was doing the same with jazz. In **The Man with the Golden Arm** (1956) he chose the medium of jazz to reflect the disturbing narrative. He says, "I wanted an element that could speak readily of hysteria and despair, an element that would localise these emotions to our country, to a large city if possible. Ergo, jazz." While the score didn't incorporate the crucial jazz ingredient – improvisation (not a happy bedfellow of split-second timing requirements) – it did incorporate the talents of two brilliant jazzers. Shorty Rogers arranged the band numbers while Shelly Manne created his own drum parts. The score was a huge success, the main title became a popular hit, and Hollywood, true to form, put into production several films with jazz scores.

The hit song was a new development for Hollywood. Three years before Bernstein's main title success, composer Dimitri Tiomkin burst into the charts with the song 'Do Not Forsake Me, Oh, My Darling' from **High Noon** (1952). In fact, the success of the song (it sold over one million copies) translated into box office triumph for the film. The result, of course, was that suddenly every major motion picture had to have a title song. Then in 1967 **The Graduate** raised serious problems for the specially composed score. The immense popularity of the songs written for the film by Paul Simon and Art Garfunkel meant that the soundtrack album as an idea, with its crop of pop songs and bits of rock scoring, became a prerequisite sales and marketing opportunity. Soon, respected composers like Bernard Herrmann and Miklos Rosza found themselves out of work and moved to Europe, where they felt they were treated with more respect. But the soundtrack album was now considered at the planning stage of a film, such was its money-spinning potential.

Today the film soundtrack has assimilated all these developments. Album, hit songs and score co-exist more comfortably. Younger composers have often grown up with pop music and do not necessarily view it with suspicion. Indeed pop elements and instrumentation are now firmly part of the composer's armoury. In a score like **American Beauty** (1999) Thomas Newman's eclectic instrumental textures integrate perfectly with the ten selected songs, while the balance of dramatic tension is not disturbed. The same can be said of Gabriel Yared's more orchestral score for **The Talented Mr Ripley** (1999).

Close Encounters of the Third Kind (1977, Steven Spielberg)

The Lost World: Jurassic Park (1997, Steven Spielberg)

American Beauty (1999, Sam Mendes)

The Talented Mr Ripley (1999, Anthony Minghella)

2001: A Space Odyssey (1968, Stanley Kubrick)

With advances in computer technology the process of film scoring has substantially changed. While the aesthetics and dramatic requirements may remain the same as one hundred years ago, it is now possible to put together reasonable orchestral mock-ups with samplers, synthesizers and computer sequencers; most home studios can synchronise film to music. The whole process has become more instant, perhaps filtering down from the rapid turn-around requirements of television scoring. Gone are the days when the director would first hear his score at the orchestral recording session.

On the following pages you will read the thoughts of twelve of the most important and influential composers working in film today. Not just in Hollywood but across the world. It's evident that there is no definitive way to score a movie and that they all have very different viewpoints. Howard Shore feels that orchestration, as part of composition, is immaterial; John

Barry feels it's crucial. Michael Nyman and Zbigniew Preisner present the outsider's view to working in Hollywood, whereas Jerry Goldsmith and Danny Elfman describe life on the front-line. Elmer Bernstein and Maurice Jarre show how composing in Hollywood has changed over the years. Philip Glass, on the other hand, comes at film from the angle of established classical composer.

We start with a chapter on Bernard Herrmann. We realise that Herrmann is not alive, and we are therefore unable to present his views in his own words, but such is his enduring influence that virtually every composer we spoke to stressed the value of his contribution to the art of scoring. So many thanks to Professor Mervyn Cooke for his enlightening words on the acknowledged master.

One of the side-effects of reading about music examples is that it makes you want to listen to them. We've tried to

Titanic (1997, James Cameron)

address this situation by compiling an accompanying CD. Obviously we can't cover everything but we've settled on one track for each composer and we've tried to make each selection as pertinent as possible to points raised in the relevant chapter. Many thanks to David Stoner and Silva Screen Records for making this CD a reality.

Apart from thanking the twelve composers for sharing their insights and experiences, and contributing scores and pictures, we would also like to thank their agents, assistants, partners and everyone who has made it possible to liaise with them despite their busy schedules. Many thanks also to David Mermelstein for his valuable help and for conducting the interviews in America, namely those with Elmer Bernstein, Maurice Jarre, Jerry Goldsmith, Danny Elfman, Philip Glass and Ryuichi Sakamoto. We would also like to thank all those who have helped us with their time and advice since this project started, including Judith Burns from The Home Office in Brighton, Phil Moad and Dave McCall from The Kobal Collection and Simon Audley from The Ronald Grant Archive. Also, many thanks to the book's designers at Artmedia, Andrea Bettella and Francesca Wisniewska, for their patience as well as their fabulous layout.

Lastly we would like to express our gratitude to the editorial team at RotoVision – Zara Emerson, Erica Ffrench, Natalia Price-Cabrera and Gary French. This book has been a mammoth task – contacting and working with the contributors, and assembling, cataloguing and editing a vast amount of material. Like a feature film, the SCREENCRAFT books are the product of a collaborative effort, and without the commitment, expertise and enthusiasm of this team, the series would not be possible.

MARK RUSSELL AND JAMES YOUNG

Bernard Herrmann was born in 1911 and received a classical training in composition and conducting at New York University and the Juilliard School of Music. His early work for CBS in the 1930s led to radio collaborations with Orson Welles for the Mercury Theatre of the Air. Welles introduced him to film scoring with **Citizen Kane** in 1941, the year in which Herrmann won his only Academy Award for **The Devil**

bernard herrmann

and Daniel Webster (1941, William Dieterle). His first collaboration with Alfred Hitchcock was in 1955. It was for Hitchcock that he would produce some of the most inventive film scores of the century, including **Vertigo** (1958), **North by Northwest** (1959) and **Psycho** (1960). Herrmann's style was equally suitable for the fantasy/science-fiction films he worked on during the 1950s and '60s, which include **The Day the Earth Stood Still** (1951, Robert Wise) and **Journey to the Centre of the Earth** (1959, Henry Levin). After the breakdown of his ten-year creative partnership with Hitchcock, he became disillusioned with Hollywood's commercial bias. After collaborating with the French *nouvelle vague* director François Truffaut on **Fahrenheit 451** (1966) and **The Bride Wore Black** (1967), Herrmann moved to the U.K. in 1972. He died on 24th December 1975, shortly after attending the final recording session of his score to Martin Scorsese's **Taxi Driver** (1976).

Bernard Herrmann was arguably the most influential of the film composers whose work came to prominence after the first decade of the sound film. Along with other native American talents such as Aaron Copland and Leonard Rosenman, Herrmann injected a much-needed dose of modernism into mainstream film scoring and opened up creative possibilities that would be exploited by numerous younger composers.

Hollywood scores of the Golden Age relied heavily on the techniques of classical music in the romantic and impressionist eras: the music was essentially narrative in function, strictly subordinate to both dialogue and visual image, and mostly based on the leitmotif, the structure of Wagnerian opera. The harmonic language was fundamentally tonal, lagging several decades behind the more advanced harmonic idioms of modern concert composers, but ideally suited to the expression of the predictable emotions of melodrama. With Herrmann's work in the 1940s and 1950s, all this began to change: comforting tonal harmonies gave way to acerbic dissonances (influenced by contemporary composers such as Stravinsky); extended melodies were abandoned in favour of brief and repetitive motivic patterns; and experimentation with tone colours and unorthodox instrumentation resulted in innovative and unpredictable musical textures.

Herrmann was fortunate in working, for the most part, with a succession of directors who respected his artistic integrity and allowed his distinctive style to develop without exerting undue pressure on him to conform to commercial formulae. Orson Welles, Alfred Hitchcock and François Truffaut all involved him in discussions of their projects at an early stage, and accorded his musical ideas a respect sadly lacking in many composer/director collaborations. In the case of Herrmann's first film score, for Welles' **Citizen Kane** (1941), this respect was demonstrated by the fact that certain sequences were edited to pre-composed music. Memorable cues include the set of variations accompanying the montage depicting the breakdown of Kane's first marriage, and the miniature dance movements underscoring events in the newspaper office. Here Herrmann demonstrated how pre-existing musical forms could be adapted for the cinema without being accorded undue prominence: the structures neatly complement the action on screen while retaining a certain degree of structural autonomy.

Both **Citizen Kane** and his next Welles project, **The Magnificent Ambersons** (1942), used fairly conventional thematic transformations to highlight narrative events. But when Herrmann began to devote more sustained attention to film work in the early 1950s, his style changed markedly. His first significant achievement was the development of an idiom tailored to suit the fantasy and science-fiction screenplays then on the increase. Herrmann's penchant for unorthodox instrumentation (nurtured by his earlier work with Welles in experimental radio drama) became the perfect tool for creating other-worldly sonorities that were light years removed from standard orchestration. As Herrmann once pointed out with incontestable logic, there is no rationale in feeling bound to use a conventional symphony orchestra for film scores which, by their very nature, are only performed once – in the recording studio.

This philosophy led to a succession of bizarre but always telling instrumental combinations, in which electronics played a prominent and pioneering role. As early as **The Devil and Daniel Webster** (1941), for which Herrmann received his only Academy Award, the Satanic elements were reinforced by experimental recording techniques combined with animated sound (artificial musical effects created by painting directly onto the celluloid soundtrack). In **The Day the Earth Stood Still** (1951), Herrmann employed two theremins – an early electronic instrument previously featured in certain films noirs – alongside electric bass, electric guitar, electric violin, three organs and multiple brass and percussion. No fewer than nine harps were heard on the soundtrack to **Beneath the 12-Mile Reef**, and multiple drummers dominated **King of the Khyber Rifles** (1953).

1

4

2

5

3

6

(1–4) **Citizen Kane**: Herrmann's debut film score involved the composer in a close collaboration with Welles at both shooting and editing stages. Herrmann conducted the score at the RKO studios, and several sequences were edited to pre-recorded music. (5–6) **The Magnificent Ambersons**: Over half an hour of Herrmann's music for his second Welles picture was cut by studio executives while the director was absent. Much of the film's music when finally released was composed by Roy Webb, and Herrmann was not consulted.

film music

(1) **Beneath the 12-Mile Reef**: Herrmann's score provided a vivid underwater soundscape. (2) **The Day the Earth Stood Still**: An early experiment in electronic techniques and idiosyncratic instrumentation, Herrmann's music captured the novelty of the robot Gort and his passengers from outer space. (3) **Journey to the Centre of the Earth**: Herrmann used a rare wind instrument called the serpent to suggest the dark depths of Jules Verne's fantasy. (4) **Jason and the Argonauts**: This film from 1963 was one of Herrmann's many collaborations with animator Ray Harryhausen.

6

7

8

(5) **The Wrong Man**: In his third collaboration with Hitchcock, Herrmann avoided lyrical music in favour of a cold precision and occasionally violent expressionism which perfectly matched the fluctuating moods of the drama. (6–7) **Cape Fear**: When Martin Scorsese remade this 1962 chiller in 1991 he retained several elements of the original, including Herrmann's score. (8) **The Devil and Daniel Webster**: Herrmann's highly experimental music won him an Oscar for this score in 1941.

1

3

2

4

(2–5) **Psycho**: Hitchcock had little confidence in the potential of his most famous project, and at one time contemplated downgrading it into a television drama. Herrmann's brilliant music – by turns brooding and violent – transformed the venture by injecting the tale with dark poetry and sinister resonance that linger in the mind long after the film's final image has faded from sight. (1) **Carrie**: Herrmann wrote several scores for films by Brian de Palma, who later paid tribute to the composer's celebrated music for **Psycho**'s notorious shower scene in his horror movie **Carrie** (1976).

5

Five organs were featured in **Journey to the Centre of the Earth** (1959), a score from which the strings were boldly omitted altogether. Unorthodox orchestrations such as these ensured that each Herrmann score had its own sonorous identity, and in this respect his work set a formidable standard of inventiveness.

It was Herrmann's ten-year collaboration with Hitchcock that allowed him to develop compositional techniques that remain influential even today. **The Wrong Man** (1957) was the first Hitchcock project to showcase Herrmann's ability to create music of claustrophobia and oppression. These distinctive atmospheres were developed in three sophisticated Hitchcock scores, now considered to be amongst the finest film music ever composed: **Vertigo** (1958), **North by Northwest** (1959) and **Psycho** (1960). In all three, the starkly abstract graphics of the main title sequences, designed by Saul Bass, allowed Herrmann free rein in setting the mood of the picture to come. While in some respects these 'overtures' were a thoroughly conventional idea (Herrmann famously reacted with horror when Brian de Palma suggested that **Sisters** (1973) should commence without mood-setting music), the compositional techniques they employed were idiosyncratic.

Most prominent was Herrmann's heavy reliance on ostinato (a label applied to any short, repeated pattern of notes; the term is the Italian word for obstinate). In Herrmann's Hitchcock scores, ostinato figurations stubbornly refuse to transform themselves into conventional melodies: instead, the fragmentary repeating patterns are formed into kaleidoscopic

musical textures that tread a precarious middle ground between stability and instability. The sense of instability is conveyed primarily by a dissonant harmonic language that persistently avoids resolution into familiar concords, even at the end of long cues: the title sequence of **North by Northwest**, for example, ends without resolution, while the conclusion of **Psycho** is accompanied by an unresolved dissonance that can only leave the viewer uncomfortable. In handling both ostinato and harmonic elements, Herrmann skilfully manipulates the audience's responses: the listener is encouraged to think that an extended melody or harmonic resolution is imminent, but it never (or rarely) comes. Without the visual image, a listener to Herrmann's music might feel constantly cheated, but in its cinematic context this inconclusive and ambiguous music precisely achieves the desired emotional effect, and has been memorably described by Royal S. Brown as "music of the irrational".

Herrmann's score to **Psycho** is universally acknowledged as one of the most original and influential in cinema history. Another example of unorthodox scoring in its exclusive use of strings (often said, perhaps fancifully, to complement the monochrome visual image), the **Psycho** music brings the simple yet intense techniques of Herrmann's earlier work to saturation point. Most celebrated of all is the famous shower scene, which Hitchcock originally intended to play without music; Herrmann persuaded him to think otherwise (the director later bluntly commenting that his proposal not to have music had been an "improper suggestion"). So novel were the screeching and slithering string glissandos

1

5

2

6

3

4

(1–6) **North by Northwest**: (3) In one scene on board a train, what at first appears to be canned music in the restaurant car is subtly transformed into lushly romantic underscoring as it gradually lends support to the flirtatious dialogue between Cary Grant and Eva Marie Saint. (6) Like all good composers, Herrmann knew when silence could be more effective than music: in this film he supplied no music for the climactic aeroplane sequence until the moment when the plane crashes into the ground. (7–8) **Vertigo**: Herrmann's music experimented boldly with unresolved dissonances and kaleidoscopic figurations ideally suited to the film's disquieting subject matter. By the late 1950s Herrmann's responses to Hitchcock's requirements had become so consistent that there are many obvious similarities in the thematic and harmonic ideas he evolved for both **Vertigo** and **North by Northwest**.

accompanying Janet Leigh's watery demise that some critics at the time thought they were electronically generated, while the sheer brutality of the music led others into thinking the scene to be far more gruesome than it really is in visual terms. Among the many self-confessed imitations of the **Psycho** score was that in de Palma's **Carrie** (1976), for which Herrmann's music had served as a temp track. The legendary shower scene has overshadowed subtler elements of Herrmann's score, such as the precise synchronisation of the doom-laden pulsating music with the action of the windscreen wipers of Leigh's car as she drives through the night. There is nothing inherently disturbing about the way in which this car journey is photographed: without the panic-stricken music, as Herrmann himself observed, Leigh could just as well be on her way to a supermarket as fleeing from a crime.

Hitchcock and Herrmann parted company when the latter's music to **Torn Curtain** (1966) was rejected by the director, ostensibly because he desired a pop score which Herrmann was unwilling to provide. This pretext masked the real reason for the rupture, which was a combination of Herrmann's distrust of what he saw as Hitchcock's sell-out to commercial interests, and the director's uncomfortable realisation that Herrmann's music had, in the opinion of many, been the defining factor behind the success of his greatest films. As French director Claude Chabrol put it, "once Hitchcock got rid of Herrmann, Hitchcock's music was good only when it was imitating Herrmann". Hitchcock had been a potent influence on certain French directors, and it was appropriate that Herrmann went on to compose two memorable scores for

Truffaut, **Fahrenheit 451** (1966) and **The Bride Wore Black** (1967). His music for the futuristic Ray Bradbury story **Fahrenheit 451**, in particular, is brilliantly inventive. Especially impressive is the mechanical march accompanying the shots of the futuristic fire engine as its crew heads impassively off to burn yet more books. Instead of the anxious, exciting music we might expect to accompany such an image, we hear clinical precision, with a quirky xylophone melody, almost childlike in its naïvety. (Given the insight into the story that Herrmann shows here, it is odd that he was so critical of the flamboyant waltz composed by Richard Rodney Bennett to characterise the luxurious train in **Murder on the Orient Express** (1974, Sidney Lumet). According to Jerry Goldsmith, Herrmann felt the suave melody to be much too flippant for a "train of death".) Truffaut had employed Herrmann on **Fahrenheit 451** because he wanted his futuristic vision to be accompanied by music of clarity and almost neo-classical simplicity – all the more effective for the contrast it creates when juxtaposed with the tender and lyrical love music that is finally allowed to dominate the underscore. After the project was complete, Truffaut wrote to Herrmann to thank him for "humanising my picture".

Herrmann's final score was for Martin Scorsese's **Taxi Driver** (1976), which featured a sultry blues theme that paid tribute to the long-standing cinematic tradition of equating jazz with urban decay and corruption. Scorsese praised Herrmann's success in establishing the psychological basis of the entire film, and the music's combination of jazz with sometimes violent modernistic elements seemed to presage a new

1

2

3

4

5

(1, 4) **The Bride Wore Black:**
Truffaut's distinctive combination of
elements inspired by Hitchcock and
Renoir elicited from Herrmann a score
in which the musical shapes often
mirror the fluid camera movements.
(2, 3, 5) **Fahrenheit 451:** The almost
toy-like fire engine in Truffaut's
nightmarish vision of a future world
deprived of books is captured by
Herrmann's oddly chirpy music.

1

5

2

3

4

(1–5) **Taxi Driver**: Herrmann's last score proved to be one of his most hauntingly memorable. Its searing blues-tinged saxophone theme had originally been written as "source music", intended to be played as a realistic part of the action, but the composer adopted it as the mainstay of his background score and conjured up a sound-world that disconcertingly combined the sleazy and the profound. In its unique combination of violent dissonance, jazz and atmospheric impressionism, Herrmann's music was a fitting conclusion to a career distinguished by the composer's consistent ability to penetrate to the psychological heart of a drama and encapsulate it in music of economy and originality. (left) Bernard Herrmann conducting at a recording session.

direction in Herrmann's style. The idea grew naturally from his earlier experiments in fusing Latin dance rhythms with advanced harmonic and rhythmic techniques (as in the main title music for **The Wrong Man**, the relentless fandango of the title sequence in **North by Northwest**, or the lilting but disquieting habañera that conjures up the aura of the ghostly Carlotta in **Vertigo**). This fusion of the popular and avant-garde was another of Herrmann's enduring legacies to subsequent film composers, and the combination of Scorsese's haunting close-ups of a yellow cab cruising the streets of New York at night and Herrmann's brooding music constitutes one of the high points of film scoring in the 1970s.

Perhaps even more important to younger composers than Herrmann's innovative compositional techniques was the realisation that, with work of such consistent and uncompromising quality, film music had at last come of age. Herrmann saw no distinction between composing concert music and working for the movies, and declared that "America is the only country in the world with so-called 'film composers' – every other country has composers who sometimes do films". His commitments in the classical arena as both composer and conductor forced him to work on a strictly limited number of film projects, but he always approached his film commissions with undiminished artistic standards and refused to compromise those standards in the face of commercial pressure. His disgust at the motion-picture industry's refusal to accord film composers the respect and recognition he felt they deserved led to his resignation from the Academy of Motion Picture Arts and Sciences.

Herrmann's influence thus persists both in terms of specific scoring methods and in his almost mythical status as a composer able to command the respect (not to say dread) of the directors with whom he worked. His cutting remarks on producers ("musical ignoramuses"), directors ("they really have no taste at all... I'd rather not do a film than have to take what a director says"), and even Hitchcock ("he only finishes a picture 60 per cent: I have to finish it for him") may not have endeared him to the Hollywood moguls, but the steady stream of artistic successes produced by his stubbornness has ensured that he has remained a potent role model for a new generation of film composers. Herrmann felt music to be "the communicating link between the screen and the audience", and in exploiting this link with such constant resourcefulness he showed how the composer, not the director, could sometimes be a film's true auteur.

MERVYN COOKE

biography

Elmer Bernstein, born in New York City in 1922, was classically trained, and is indisputably one of the giants of film music. His scores are recognised for their rhythmic intensity and strong emphasis on melody. The great stylistic range of his work always manages to serve the dramatic purpose of the film while at the same time retaining his own unique identity as one of film music's most creative voices.

elmer bernstein

His early grounding in compositional method, notably with Aaron Copland and Stefan Wolpe, ensured that he was equally at home with the European tradition as well as with 20th-century American modernism. He has been nominated for 13 Academy Awards and awarded an Oscar for his original score to **Thoroughly Modern Millie** (1967, George Hill). He has worked with a wide range of directors, among them David Miller (**Saturday's Hero**, 1951), Otto Preminger (**The Man with the Golden Arm**, 1956) and Cecil B. De Mille (**The Ten Commandments**, 1956). He has written scores for many genre of film: **The Magnificent Seven** (1960, John Sturges); **Walk on the Wild Side** (1962, Edward Dmytryk); **To Kill a Mockingbird** (1962, Robert Mulligan) and **The Great Escape** (1963, John Sturges). More recently, Bernstein has worked extensively with director Martin Scorsese on films including **Cape Fear** (1991), **The Age of Innocence** (1993) and **Bringing out the Dead** (1999).

interview

I grew up in New York City. My parents were interested in the arts. My mother studied dance with Isadora Duncan and my father was a really good amateur singer. I started piano lessons at the age of nine and I decided around 12 years old that I wanted to do something with music. I began studying with Aaron Copland. He decided that I needed some more basic training and so I studied with the composer Israel Citkowitz, and then later with Roger Sessions and ultimately, with the man from whom I learned the most, Stefan Wolpe. My involvement with movies happened by accident. I was serving in the army air force in the Second World War and was assigned to Special Services, propaganda broadcasts. They wanted a folk song on each of the propaganda shows and as I knew something about American folk music, I was brought in as arranger. When the fellow who wrote the background scores for the shows absented himself and the director called me in and asked if I could do it I said, "certainly".

1

2

(1–4) **The Man with the Golden Arm**: By opting for a jazz score instead of the usual symphonic score, Bernstein broke new ground with this film: "It just seemed the appropriate thing to do – it was a film about a junkie who wanted to be a jazz drummer." (2) Silence was adopted for some of the card scenes: "There used to be a tendency until the late '30s to have music wall-to-wall. Then composers like Bernard Herrmann began making the music dramatically precise, as well as functional." (4) "Kim Novak had a gentle kind of sadness – an important factor for me in the creation of her theme. Drama without humour is boring and violence without the sense of sadness that accompanies it goes beyond boring."

1

2

6

4

5

(1–6) **The Ten Commandments**: Bernstein was 34 when he composed for his first Hollywood epic. His score is richly thematic and dramatic, and unusually for film music dealing with a biblical subject he doesn't use a heavenly choir. "The God theme. That was a very big problem!" (1–2) The opening two pages of Bernstein's 'End Title' music. This is the conductor's score, hence the condensed orchestration. Note the orchestrator's credit (Lucien Cailliet) and the handwritten instruction from the recording session 'Please save Take 6 – complete take'. Presumably many versions were recorded and version number six was the preferred choice for the soundtrack.

After the war I worked on a musical radio show. Sometime later one of my mates from the army wrote a book which he sold to the movies, and he also sold me to the producer of the movie. So I went to Hollywood in 1950 and did the score for a film called **Saturday's Hero** (1951). That was my first film and after that I stayed on in L.A. I think the studio system was superior to what's going on now, especially for young people, because you were given a chance to learn something. You weren't given a major film right away but you could get into the system and learn your craft at the feet of giants like Bernard Herrmann, Franz Waxman, and Max Steiner.

In 1952 I did a film called **Sudden Fear** which had a score that was unusual for the time, in that it relied heavily on solo woodwind instruments. Film scoring in those days was a symphonic, big orchestra kind of thing. The car chase in the movie consisted of a big piece for two pianos and orchestra which again was unusual for the time, as the piano was considered to be a parlour instrument. This attracted some attention, and there was a screening to which we invited John Green of Metro, Roy Piesta, Head of Music at Paramount and Igor Preminger, a prominent agent. He was Otto's brother. Three years later Otto was making **The Man with the Golden Arm**. Igor remembered the score for **Sudden Fear** and suggested he should look me up. "Who the hell is he?" said Otto. Igor suggested he call John Green at Metro and John, God bless him, gave me a terrific send-off. So Otto hired me. After being hired I remember going into Otto's office one day and saying to him, "You know, I have an idea about the way I want to do this film, but I thought I might tell you before

you throw me out of here". He asked, "Well, what is it?" I said, "Think of it as a score for a jazz orchestra rather than a symphony orchestra". So Otto said something you would never hear today: "That's what I hired you for. If that's what you think then you should go do it!" When I made the suggestion I had no idea it was going to be so sensationally ground-breaking. It just seemed to be the appropriate thing to do. After all, it was a film about a junkie who wanted to be a jazz drummer. I am not a jazz player although I was brought up with the music. I worked with a team of arrangers, Jack Hayes and Leo Schuken, when the band was playing along with the orchestra. Where the band is playing solo the arrangements are by Shorty Rogers. There's also a drug withdrawal scene which features drums very prominently and which depended very much on Shelly Manne's improvisation. We all worked together on this. We had a good time.

I didn't really know about drug dependency in those days but what I was conscious of was that there was an aura of sadness over the whole thing. Kim Novak had that gentle sadness. There are times when I'm affected by things that are not directly musical, in this case it was her character's name, "Molly". Those two syllables, the first two notes of the music, linked to her character which starts as a piano theme and then goes into the flute, are linked to the name "Molly". It was the same thing with the first two notes of **The Magnificent Seven** – you could hear the word "Seven". After the magnanimous "You do what you think is right", Preminger began to ask questions. He could be very tough. He wanted to know what it was going to sound like. Finally,

1

2

3

(1–3) **The Magnificent Seven**: (2) The 'Overture', containing the famous main theme. (3) 'Harry's Mistake': Spanish-American dances mix with urgent action music and prominent percussion – one of Bernstein's most inventive scores.

after a few weeks of this, Shelly Manne and I made a recording with me on piano. Preminger was fine with that. Some directors are much more intrusive, to their own discredit. If you hire a composer who's worth anything, the best thing he's going to do is contribute something that the director couldn't even think of. It's another world. If Otto had used a temp score of something that was not jazz and said, "this is what I want", then he'd never have had that jazz score for **The Man with the Golden Arm**.

When I came to do **The Ten Commandments**, De Mille initially kept me on week-to-week. It began as a composing job to write the 'Egyptian Girls' Dance'. Victor Young was supposed to do the scoring but he was terminally ill and he said there was no way he could do the film and so he said to me, "be my guest". De Mille needed more things: more dances, more pieces for harps or flutes etc. Eventually he asked me to write some themes and that was it, fixed. I did the entire movie. I don't think anybody ever knew more about making a film than Cecil B. De Mille. He crossed every t and dotted every i. He approved every single costume, including what he wanted for the extras. There was no indecision. The film opens with an overture which precedes an appearance by De Mille himself. I had in mind the atmosphere of nostalgically old Hollywood, a sense of Hollywood theatre. The main theme throughout the film, God's theme, was a big problem. When De Mille specifically wanted me to make a theme it was the hardest thing to get to. I spent a lot of time on that, maybe an entire month, something you would not be able to do any more. Historically **The Ten Commandments**

was very hard. Who knows what they played? We would be brought authentic Egyptian instruments which we could listen to. They were still playable. You'd have a sense of the instruments, but not of the music. That was doubly so for the Hebrews. We had no idea, so I just started inventing. De Mille would listen to the pieces played on the piano, maybe not to every single note. He wasn't so worried about orchestration, more about thematic use. He had a very Wagnerian idea that the themes followed the characters and identified them. The whole movie has a no-holds-barred presentation because De Mille always thought big in an unremitting style. It never excuses itself at any point, and it tends to take you with it.

The Magnificent Seven score really benefited from the fact that for years I'd wanted to do an American type of theme as it was something I knew a great deal about, partly because of my own interest in American folk music, and also because of my relationship with Copland. He invented American music to a great degree – a certain style, a certain sound, and I always found it very attractive. Originally I'd wanted to do the score for **The Big Country**, which was done by Jerome Moross and a beautiful and magnificent score it was. By the time I got to do **The Magnificent Seven** all of this stuff that had been in my head for years and years had a chance to be set free, and I think that accounts for the tremendous amount of energy and rhythmic intensity in that score. The influence was Tex Mex, and I also brought in a lot of characteristically Mexican percussion instruments, and guitar. However, I wasn't drawing on folk themes – I was drawing on feelings.

1

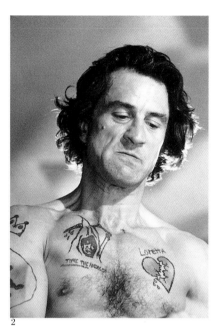

(1) **Cape Fear**: Bernard Herrmann wrote the original score for the 1962 film by J. Lee Thompson. The film is an exercise in terror, telling of a family whose peaceful lives are transformed into a nightmare of fear through a psychopathic ex-convict.

(2–3) **Cape Fear**: For Martin Scorsese's remake in 1991 Bernstein worked closely with Herrmann's score: "Herrmann's music is not necessarily in the same place as where it was in the first film. He came across like a prophet to me – his score in the Scorsese film was more pertinent 30 years later than it was in the original movie."

elmer bernstein

2

3

film music

1

2

3

(1–3) **The Age of Innocence:**
Described by critics as the most
violent movie Martin Scorsese ever
made, although for its emotional and
psychological, rather than physical
violence. Bernstein's score aimed to
capture the stifling but refined
elegance of the era, incorporating
many waltz themes. (2) "The scene
where Michelle Pfeiffer and Winona
Ryder are watching the opera at the
beginning of the film is, as far as I am
concerned, the most interesting piece
of scoring in the film. On the one hand
we are hearing the music of the opera,
and on the other hand, the scoring
music introduces a very thin, nervous
element which addresses itself to a
sense of discomfort."

I'm also a great believer in silence as part of the design. A film score is a part of the general sound design of the film and the areas you don't have music are just as important as the areas where you decide to score. In the early days of film scoring there was a tendency to have music wall-to-wall. Then, with the emergence of people like Bernard Herrmann, who came with a peculiarly American voice, the music became more dramatically precise. I told Martin Scorsese that Herrmann is one of my idols and I would really like to spend some time working with his old score for **Cape Fear**. I probably only wrote about ten minutes of music for that film. The first half of the main title was me but basically it's Herrmann. What's interesting is that his music is not necessarily in the same place as in the original film. But the thing that thrilled me was that Herrmann came across like a prophet in the sense that I thought his score in the Scorsese film was more pertinent 30 years later than it was in the original movie. Actually I don't write much like Herrmann because I'm more of a melodic composer. But what I did learn from him, and which I didn't necessarily have the instinct to do, is to repeat things a lot, to be really economical. I also learnt his use of low-end instruments which he employed frequently – for example alto flute, bass flute, the contrabass clarinet. Those low woodwinds can be very effective.

Scorsese is one of those directors who will talk through the sequences and the way he would like the music. He said that listening to music is what made him want to become a director. For him the image and the music are inseparable. He finds it very difficult to edit a film cold, so he will tend to bring in the music as he's editing the film. In the case of **The Age of Innocence**, I wrote some themes for him which he liked and I then suggested that we make a temp score based on these themes, so he was always working with what became the final score.

I've been blessed in my life. I was lucky to be there in the '50s, the halcyon days of film scoring. Even though the art of film music is in an abysmal state in the United States, with music designed to be specifically commercial rather than germane to the dramatic work, it'll probably turn itself around. These things usually do – I'm an optimist.

elmer bernstein

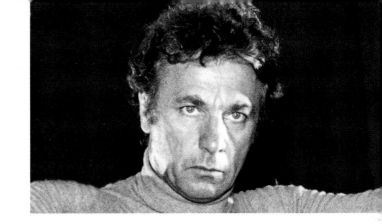

Maurice Jarre was born in Lyons, France, in September 1924. He worked as musical director of the Théâtre National Populaire in Paris for 12 years before becoming a full-time film composer. His early scores were for short features by young French directors of the time such as Resnais and Franju before moving on to large scale international productions. Arriving in L.A. in 1964, his attitude to film

maurice jarre

scoring was radically different from the old Hollywood style of grand orchestral gestures, favouring a more restrained, almost chamber approach, often incorporating electronic sounds and *musique concrète*. Jarre has won three Academy Awards for his scores to **Lawrence of Arabia**, **Doctor Zhivago** and **A Passage to India**. Early French films he wrote scores for include **Hôtel des Invalides** (1952, Georges Franju) and **Les Dimanches de Ville d'Avray** (1962, Serge Bourguignon). Jarre has enjoyed long-running relationships with directors David Lean and Peter Weir. For the former, Jarre composed the music for arguably three of the most famous and well-loved films ever made: **Lawrence of Arabia** (1962), **Doctor Zhivago** (1965) and **A Passage to India** (1984). He has written scores for a significant number of Peter Weir's films including **The Year of Living Dangerously** (1982), **Witness** (1985) and **Dead Poets Society** (1989). His filmography is extensive, including among others **Fatal Attraction** (1987, Adrian Lyne).

I was born in Lyons. My parents were not musical. My father was the technical director of broadcast radio in France and one day he came back from the radio station with some records. I played one, the second 'Hungarian Rhapsody' by Liszt recorded and arranged by Stokowski and the Philadelphia Orchestra. Suddenly I had discovered something – the sound, everything. Immediately I wanted to become a conductor. However, I was 16 years old and it was too late to become a conductor or violinist or clarinet player. It would have taken 15 years for me to have become a decent player. So I was advised to take up percussion. I worked really hard and was admitted to the Paris Conservatoire.

I became quite a good percussionist and got a job with the Jean-Louis Barrault Company. He wanted two musicians to play the music for his productions. The other was Pierre Boulez. The two of us played together for four years, me on all percussion instruments from timpani to xylophone and Pierre

1

2

3

4

5

(1–3) **Lawrence of Arabia**: "I tried to find a beautiful, idealistic theme for this film. I think it is very important to have a main theme and to manage to make as many variations as possible instead of disturbing the audience with too many different themes which then become lost." (3) Watching the initial 40-hour screening gave Jarre the inspiration for the score: "I was totally, absolutely amazed by the beauty of the desert – you feel the sand, you feel the heat." (4) The director David Lean in conversation with Maurice Jarre. "I learned a lot from David Lean. He knew where the music should start growing and where it should fade out. Sometimes he even put the beginnings and endings of music in the script." (5) Maurice Jarre working on the film's score.

playing piano and Ondes Martenot. When we needed other instruments, such as trumpets for example, we used a record player with the needle in the band. We were just two crazy guys rushing from here to there with the sound bubbling over so that the audience thought it was a big orchestra. It truly was a wonderful time.

Then I was invited by Jean Vilar to write the music for a play, Kleist's 'Prince Of Homburg', which was being performed at the Avignon Festival. This was my first real composition. I was also the conductor and I decided to place the musicians differently: some would play behind the audience for the battle scene. It was a big success. When we came back to Paris, Jean became director of the Théâtre National Populaire and he asked me to be musical director. I stayed for 12 years and wrote music for about 70 different plays – Molière, Shakespeare, Brecht, O'Neill. I had 30 musicians to work with every night. It was a great exercise in both orchestration and conducting.

In 1952 I did my first feature, a short called **Hôtel des Invalides**. I started to do more films in France with young directors like Alain Resnais and Jacques Demy. Then in 1962 I did a film for Serge Bourguignon called **Les Dimanches de Ville d'Avray**. Sam Spiegel, the producer, saw this and he liked the music. He wanted to see me. He said, "I just did the biggest production ever made, a film about Lawrence of Arabia and because it's the biggest I want three composers". I asked who they would be. "I want Khatchaturian to write the Arabic music." I said this was strange to ask a Russian

Armenian to write Arabic music. Then he said, "I want Benjamin Britten to write the British music". That made sense. "But what do you want me to do?", I asked. "You will write the programme music and do the orchestration." I was young so I was happy just to be able to write music in the company of Britten and Khatchaturian. Spiegel suggested I come to London to see the film as they'd just finished shooting in Jordan and Morocco, so I got all the books I could on the subject and began research.

The first screening was on a Monday at nine o' clock. David Lean wasn't there as he was busy editing. After three hours I had only seen beautiful, spectacular film of the desert, no Peter O'Toole, no Omar Sharif. So Spiegel said I should come back at two and we'd continue. By six o' clock there was still no O'Toole or Sharif, only desert and a few camels. By the Thursday, after 40 hours of film, I finally saw Peter O'Toole. I said, "My God, this is three or four films". Spiegel said that Lean knew exactly what he was doing and that he would cut the film down to about four hours. This was July and there were only six months to go before the premiere opened in front of the Queen.

I was concerned about the technical process of putting music to film. Then Spiegel said that Khatchaturian couldn't leave Russia and that Britten wanted a year and a half to write his share because he had some other project. Spiegel suggested that I should continue to work on it because he had to return to the States. Then, in the middle of August, he called me to say that he had good news and had made a deal with an

(1–3) **Doctor Zhivago**: (2) Jarre initially wanted to use a balalaika orchestra for Lara's theme but L. A. was unable to supply one. However, he did find a Russian community: "I went to the Orthodox church and asked a guy if he could play the balalaika. He said yes, he could get another 25 to 30 players. They all played by ear. On the recording I was miming the rhythm and they followed my lips."

(1–3) **Doctor Zhivago**: "David Lean said that in a way the film composer is like a doctor. Sometimes you can repair a bad cut but at other times the patient is dead. If the director is not confident when he is shooting and he thinks the music will help, he's wrong. It's better sometimes to have silence because the music should always arrive at the right moment and for the right reason." The music department at MGM was initially sceptical of David Lean's choice of Jarre for this score, saying they had "better composers for Russia and snow".

American composer, Richard Rodgers, to write 90 per cent of the score leaving me the remaining ten per cent. I liked Richard Rodgers but he seemed a strange choice. Furthermore, Spiegel said that Rodgers wouldn't be coming to London to view the film as he knew the story and would simply send some themes for me to arrange. I was stupefied.

In the middle of September there was a meeting at which I would finally get to meet David Lean and also hear Rodgers' themes played by a pianist. I was very impressed by Lean – he had a lot of class, very British, very cool. "Nice to meet you", and that's it. The pianist began to play the love theme, then the Arabic theme, then an English military march, at which point Lean jumped up saying, "You stopped me from work to listen to this? It has nothing to do with Lawrence of Arabia!" So Spiegel turned to me in an accusing voice – "Well, you didn't bring anything to show us!" I said that I did have something and that I could give him an idea of it, although I was not a pianist.

The first thing I played was Lawrence's theme and before I finished I felt David's hand touch my shoulder. "That's exactly what I want, Sam. This young chap should write the music and we should help him." I couldn't believe it! To tell the truth, I still feel the hand of David on my shoulder to this day. Then David told me that the work might be difficult for me because he had started to edit the second part first. I would have to begin there and imagine what I was going to do in the first part, plus I had to do it all in six weeks. I knew the basis of the music would be percussion and strange instruments like the Ondes Martenot. Sometimes the keyboard was not used as a melody instrument but played at the bottom in tone clusters so that the piano became a bass percussion instrument. I didn't use any Arabic instruments. It was music from a Western point of view about Arabia, not from the inside. I had come to the Lawrence theme by researching the life and realising what a human person he was as well as being very idealistic. Also after having seen those 40 hours of film I was amazed by how beautiful the desert was. In fact I had the feeling that I wasn't in the desert but somewhere dreamy yet realistic also, as if I could feel the heat and the sand. I got the feel for the theme right away and I didn't change one note from the beginning. The same thing happened with **Doctor Zhivago**, although the process of arriving at that point was more painful.

After **Lawrence Of Arabia**, Lean went to India to rest and he lost my connection as I'd moved to the USA. When he began work on **Doctor Zhivago** he tried to find me by calling the music department at MGM. The guy said, "What do you want Maurice for, Mr. Lean? He's very good for open space and desert but we have better composers for Russia and snow." Incredible! It was all part of the studio bureaucracy. In each studio there was a guy who specialised in main titles, even if you had different composers there was always a special orchestrator. If you listen, all the main titles of that period sound a little bit alike. Big sound, big themes, big orchestra. I arrived in 1964, during the last few months of the old Hollywood style.

1

2

3

4

5

(1–6) **Witness**: This film score was a departure for Jarre from conventional orchestration. He felt that an orchestra would create a sentimental feeling whereas he wanted to create a cold, alienating atmosphere: "Also, the Amish people do not like instrumental music. Electronic music was the most interesting and logical choice, as it doesn't have that acoustical sound." (6) Jarre tried to "go against the picture" with a heavy organ sound when Kelly McGillis and Harrison Ford finally kiss: "An electronic violin would have been the worst thing."

6

1

2

(1–3) **Dead Poets Society**: (1) Jarre used Beethoven's 'Ode to Joy' as the source music for the football game where they recite poetry. (2) Jarre's moody synthesizer piece accompanies the boys when they meet in the cave. (3) The finale, 'Keating's Triumph' was especially important; Weir instructed Jarre: "Look, he didn't lose, he won. This conclusion has to be made musically."

3

Eventually David and I connected and I went to Spain where he was shooting. He had reconstructed Moscow about 15 kilometres outside Madrid. He said he'd found the perfect music for Lara's theme and he played me this beautiful old Russian song. That was fine – it meant I could concentrate on other themes in the film. But then MGM said that they couldn't clear the rights for the Russian song so David asked me to write something.

We got back to L.A. for the editing. I started to write a theme and went to present it to David. I played it and he looked at me and said, "You can do better". I was disappointed. So I started on another. I played it. "It's too sad." Then a third. "Too fast." It was a Friday night. Lean said, "Look Maurice, I feel you're concentrating too much on Zhivago and Russia. Take the weekend off. Go with your girlfriend to the mountains and think about a love theme, not Russia, not Zhivago." Suddenly it dawned on me that I had been more or less subconsciously trying to imitate the old Russian song he had loved so much, trying to make it sound Russian. I returned on Monday and in one hour I got the love theme.

In fact Lara's theme has nothing to do with Russia. What makes it sound Russian is the balalaikas, that sweeping sound you can't get with anything else. All the orchestration is on the balalaikas, 30 of them, bass, baritone, alto, soprano. When you play it on the piano it sounds completely different. Lean had a very big input because he always knew, even at the script stage, just where the music would begin and end. I learned a lot from him.

Peter Weir has a wide cultural knowledge of different music from electronic to pop to jazz, classical, opera. For a while Weir was concentrating on electronic sound. Independently of his preference I also decided that electronic sounds would be better than orchestral music for **Witness**. Firstly, I thought that the music should be without sentimentality, so that it was almost cold, detached. Secondly, the Amish people don't want instrumental music as they say it's from the devil. Nevertheless electronic music can have a slightly acoustical sound, like an aura.

For the barn-building scene Weir had been using a temp score of the Pachelbel canon. He'd edited the scene to it so it was really difficult to replace it with my music. I studied his editing very carefully and made a sketch like a geographical plan. I started to think how the Amish have something very religious but also very straight, not sentimental. I used eight different synthesizer players. I found this fantastic instrument invented by Nyle Steiner called an Electronic Valve Instrument (EVI). It's an electronic instrument but it has a human quality as it has to be blown. When the theme comes in as Kelly McGillis and Harrison Ford finally kiss there's suddenly an organ sound. Instead of obviously using a violin I tried to go against the picture with something that was really aggressive in a way.

Whenever I see a film, a good film, I feel the orchestration right away. When I saw **The Year of Living Dangerously**, I immediately thought of the gamelan, not for local colour but as the basis of the sound. I intended to use a real gamelan but

1

3

(1–3) **Fatal Attraction**: Although this film has never been considered a classic, its impact on the film industry has been immense. It is really the first of the romance/slasher thrillers and has spawned many similarly themed films. (right) Maurice Jarre.

2

that became difficult for logistic and even political reasons, so finally I sampled each instrument of the gamelan. I worked with a great engineer in Sydney for 16 hours a day for four months. That's why there is such a unity of sound. There is an instrument on the gamelan with about 15 different sounds, gongs, all tuned – and they're all tuned differently from a Western instrument. I also used piano in places to give a subtle background texture. When you play a chord you hear the percussion sound, but if you record only the resonance it becomes something else. If you then mix different chords together it becomes a strange thing.

You know, I think when you age and become more critical it's sometimes more difficult to choose a film when you don't do it for money or glory. It has to hit something inside you. Sometimes you can make a judgement mistake – the first time you see the film finished and you start to think "I don't know if there are a lot of people who are going to see this film". And then it is a big success!

Every time I finish a film I don't want to watch it anymore or to listen to the music. I spend a lot of energy on it and I love to do it but the last time I want to see it is at the first public performance as a member of the audience. That's it.

biography

Born in L.A. in February 1929, Jerry Goldsmith is one of the world's most prolific and talented composers (he dislikes the term "film composer"). He studied with a variety of musicians including Jacob Gimpel, Mario Castelnuovo-Tedesco and Miklos Rozsa. His career began in radio and television, composing scores for popular shows such as *The Twilight Zone*, *Gunsmoke* and *The Man from U.N.C.L.E.* During a

jerry goldsmith

career that has already spanned half a century, Goldsmith has written at least 175 scores. He has enjoyed fruitful working relationships with directors Franklin Schaffner (**The Stripper**, 1963; **Planet of the Apes**, 1968; **Patton**, 1969; **Papillon**, 1973; **Islands in the Stream**, 1977; **The Boys from Brazil**, 1978) and Paul Verhoeven (**Total Recall**, 1990; **Basic Instinct**, 1992; **The Hollow Man**, 2000). Goldsmith has scored many of the truly classic films in the history of Hollywood cinema: **Chinatown** (1974, Roman Polanski); **The Omen** (1976, Richard Donner), for which he won an Academy Award; **Alien** (1979, Ridley Scott); **Poltergeist** (1982, Tobe Hopper) and **L.A. Confidential** (1997, Curtis Hanson).

interview

I'd been taking piano lessons since I was six and when I was about 12 my parents thought I was serious and decided that they would invest in a good teacher, so I started studying with Jacob Gimpel. In the 1940s L.A. was a haven for all the European intellectuals who came here to escape the war. Gimpel was a great teacher. Shortly after that, at 13, I decided I wanted to compose and my parents arranged for me to have theory lessons as well as harmony and counterpoint. Then when I was 16 I started studying composition privately with Mario Castelnuovo-Tedesco.

Tedesco was a wonderfully skilled musician and a lovely man, but he was stylistically locked in the late 19th century as a composer. I was also studying at City College with Ernst Krenick who was at the other end of the spectrum. It became confusing. You take a piece you've written to a teacher and all he can do is give you his opinion of it. Teaching composition is really a very subjective thing. You're better off analysing

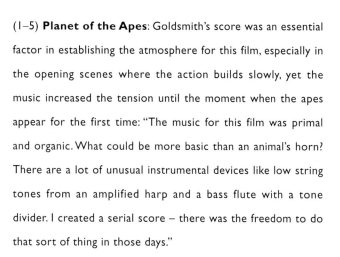

film music

(1–5) **Planet of the Apes**: Goldsmith's score was an essential factor in establishing the atmosphere for this film, especially in the opening scenes where the action builds slowly, yet the music increased the tension until the moment when the apes appear for the first time: "The music for this film was primal and organic. What could be more basic than an animal's horn? There are a lot of unusual instrumental devices like low string tones from an amplified harp and a bass flute with a tone divider. I created a serial score – there was the freedom to do that sort of thing in those days."

the Beethoven Piano Sonatas for form and structure – they're such perfection.

I wanted to compose and become immortal in the concert hall but then the pragmatic side of me took over and I realised that I didn't want to starve. At City College I worked in the opera department, the company dance classes and I was also the editor of a radio show. So I was getting a wonderful applied music background and somewhere along the line I realised that films were a way I could compose and make a living. So I got a job as a clerk at CBS and after six months I went to the head of the music department and said, "Here I am!" I showed him some things I had written and he gave me a job doing bits of everything like writing cues for radio shows. Then television started in 1955 and they needed someone young and cheap. I was doing a weekly television show with a small orchestra. You had to be inventive and very fast. There was a lot of music to be written in the hour between the dress rehearsal and going on air. We didn't have time to rehearse it. You learned to ad-lib a lot. They were wonderful times because the shows were done live – there was no filming in those days. It went out and that was it, including the mistakes.

Nowadays film-makers often come in with a predisposed idea of how they think the music should be because of this temp tracking that is constantly being done. It's a curse. Every movie is wall-to-wall with music. When I did **Planet of the Apes**, Franklin Schaffner, the director, and I talked about what I really wanted to do. There was this kind of organic feel. Schaffner was the dream director for me; we had a great and long relationship. Some of the best things I've ever done were with him: **Planet of the Apes, Patton, Papillon, Islands in the Stream, The Boys from Brazil**. Frank never heard a note of music before I came on the scoring stage. He didn't want to hear it and he never put temp music in his movies.

Paul Verhoeven, who I'm working with now, also has a great attitude. He comes to my studio and we sit and listen to everything. It's all done electronically and that's a good thing. In the old days you played the theme for the producer and the director on the piano and that was it. Then the rest of us would sort of hold our breath until we got through the first couple of tunes with the orchestra. Now I can go in and more or less spend the time making music and not worrying about it. I finished **Basic Instinct** and Paul left, and I did the recording in Europe. Paul didn't attend the recordings. I don't think he ever heard them. He just said, "That's the way it will go in the movie". And it did.

I started working with Schaffner back in the '50s in television. The first film we did was called **The Stripper**. We were both under contract to Fox. When we worked on **Planet of the Apes** Frank and I talked a lot about the music, about rocks and indigenous instruments, whatever that means. He'd call me every morning at eight o' clock to ask "Are you working? What scene are you working on?". I'd tell him and he'd make some little joke and that was it. The subject was primitive – it was fantasy, it was in the future, and so the music could be anything I wanted. So I decided on a serial score and went off and did it. In the period of the early '60s until the mid-'70s you could do anything you wanted. I don't know if you could do that today. The closest I got was when I did **Total Recall** with Verhoeven and people would say, "Where's the tune?" And I'd shake my head and tell them, "There isn't a tune, there's a theme".

As far as **Planet of the Apes** is concerned I don't really know where the music came from. I just sat down and started doing it. I had an office at Fox. I was writing on the lot and hanging out with the musicians. They knew I was always looking for things and they'd always come up with the latest gadgets. I remember a flute player in the orchestra, Abe Most, who came over with some early electronic stuff. He had a bass flute and a tone divider. You'd play one note and you'd get two. You could set it to intervals and repeat notes. It was simplistically naïve but it made interesting noises. What's interesting about the music for **Planet of the Apes** is that I've been playing it in concert recently and I don't have any of those effects. I just do it with a normal orchestra and it still sounds fine.

With **Chinatown**, the original score was not used and at the last minute Roman Polanski called me and I wrote it in ten days. I met with him and saw the picture, which had already been spotted. He talked about everything except the movie. I never saw him again. I talked to him once though. I was in London and he was with Robert Evans, the producer, and he called me and said, "That was nice music you wrote". That was the only feedback I ever had.

I actually worked with Bob Evans on **Chinatown**. He said it should have a period feel. And I said, "No. If what you see on the screen is perfect, why make it sound like the 1930s?" He asked me what I was going to do and I said, "I'm going to have an orchestra: it's going to be strings, four pianos, four harps, a solo trumpet and a little percussion". He said, "It sounds great". And I said, "It does?". He had no idea what I was talking about. It was an interesting situation because the picture had been dubbed and previewed. All the sound effects were as they were going to be. All they had to do was go back and put the music in. So I got the sound effects and I always remember that scene with this fly buzzing around Jack Nicholson. You got this arid feeling and I kept that in mind and I actually wrote around the sound of that fly.

They never heard a note of it until the scoring stage. Bob Evans was running the studio and he was head of production. He's a really good producer but he was driving me nuts. "That little note, can you get that little note?" We went on for hours. The head of the music department came and said "Can anybody out there pull the plug? I can't do it, he's head of the studio!" Still, I must say, we got a beautiful performance.

Film-makers live with temp music for months now in the editing room, so when the composer comes in they already think they know what they want for the film. Often the music that I write is in such contrast to the temp music that they don't know what to make of it. I remember with **Papillon**, the editor had put a piece of music on the very ending of the picture and Schaffner went crazy – "Get that out!".

1

2

3

(1–3) Goldsmith had only ten days to write the music for **Chinatown**: "Originally they wanted period music but I talked them off that idea. I used pianos, harps, guitars, a solo trumpet, and at one point, the shocking part of the story, the mother/sister thing, there's a low moaning sound created by rubbing a rubber ball against a hollow piece of wood." (3) The fly buzzing around Jack Nicholson in the reservoir scene gave Goldsmith an "arid feeling" which he kept in mind when writing the music for this scene: "It was wonderful to have the picture dubbed sound-effect-wise."

1

2

3

(1–6) **Alien**: This film is mostly remembered for its grisly and disturbing special effects. It also offered up some classic atmospheric situations for Goldsmith's score: "Although the score was quite romantic really." However, working on this film was not a particularly pleasant experience for Goldsmith: "As with the original score for **2001: A Space Odyssey** there were some casualties of the temp track in this film – as in the scene where the pods open."

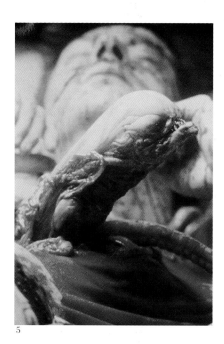

5

6

(1, 3–6) **Poltergeist**: Goldsmith's score for this film is classic horror. His score is cleverly divided between the mystic quiet scenes, those featuring Carol Anne's lullaby theme, and the loudly scored terrifying poltergeist scenes. In true horror style the music manipulates the viewer into believing that the end has been reached when Carol Anne has been rescued for the first time. (2) Jerry Goldsmith conducting.

film music

(1–3) **Basic Instinct:** Here, Goldsmith heightened the terror through a successful mix of music and silence: "The silence was essential to the structure of the piece and it gave the music a chance to breathe. There's definitely too much music in films today."

There are two casualties of temp-tracking in **Alien**. There's the scene where the pods open, where they wake from hyper sleep, and which they'd temp-tracked with some of my music from **Freud**. They all said, "Isn't that wonderful?" And I said, "No, it's terrible". It doesn't work at all. I wrote something that was really wonderful for that scene and they ended up buying in the music from **Freud**. They fell in love with the temp music. Then they took the **Freud** Symphony as the end title. What I wrote didn't work for them. I didn't want the **Freud** Symphony in there. It wasn't a happy time because the music was churned around and moved. It wasn't the way I wrote it and a lot of it was left out.

The happy art of composing for film is knowing where to play and not to play in the spotting of the music. It was always a two or three day job just to sit with the director and decide where to do it and where not. I remember it took three days with John Huston when I did **Freud**, whereas today I don't even know where to spot it because they've already spotted. There are guys now whose job is just temp-tracking movies. They even get a credit at the end of the picture!

The most significant pictures that people constantly talk about of mine are **Patton** and **Chinatown** because they were great movies to begin with. You have to start with the basic premise of a great script. Without the screenplay you haven't got anything. Plus they were so well spotted for music and there isn't that much music, which must mean something.

Something that I try to explain to my students is that I can't teach them how to score a film, how to write music for a certain scene. I may do it one way, which works fine, but they may do it another which I don't think works but a director might like. When I'm sitting and writing something I can't explain why I do it or how, it just happens. It's a feeling. Sometimes it works and sometimes it doesn't, but the more I think about it the more trouble I get into. So, I just react to what I see.

Born J. B. Prendergast in 1933 in Yorkshire, England, John Barry studied classical music and jazz before forming the John Barry Seven in the late 1950s. After several hits, and success as a composer for TV commercials, he began to work in film. He won Academy Awards for **Born Free** (1966, James Hill) (Best Score and Best Song), **The Lion in Winter** (1968, Anthony Harvey), **Out of Africa** (1985,

john barry

Sydney Pollack) and **Dances with Wolves** (1990, Kevin Costner). He received great acclaim as the composer and arranger for the highly successful Bond series, particularly **Dr No** (1962, Terence Young) for which he composed the theme. Other Bond scores by John Barry include **From Russia with Love** (1963, Terence Young); **Goldfinger** (1964, Guy Hamilton); **Thunderball** (1965, Terence Young); **You Only Live Twice** (1967, Lewis Gilbert); and **The Man with the Golden Gun** (1974, Guy Hamilton). Barry began work on low-budget, British films such as **Beat Girl** (1959, Edmond T. Gréville). He then developed a working relationship with director Bryan Forbes on a succession of films (**The L-Shaped Room**, 1962; **Seance on a Wet Afternoon**, 1964; **The Whisperers**, 1966), before writing scores for directors like Richard Lester (**The Knack**, 1965), John Schlesinger (**Midnight Cowboy**, 1969), Richard Attenborough (**Chaplin**, 1992) and Roland Joffé (**The Scarlet Letter**, 1995).

You could say I was brought up in film. My father owned eight theatres in the North of England and I remember him lifting me into the back of the stalls when I was about three and a half years old and seeing this big black-and-white mouse on the screen, which was the early version of Mickey Mouse. Subconsciously I think I paid particular attention to the music from very early on. I studied piano at school and when I left I studied harmony and counterpoint with Dr Francis Jackson, the organist and choir master at York Minster. I learned the trumpet and played in a dance band three nights a week, while I was also doing publicity for my father for the eight theatres. I also did a correspondence course at that time called 'The Joseph Schillinger System of Music by Maths'. Schillinger was a Russian immigrant who taught in New York. Gershwin, Benny Goodman and Glenn Miller all studied with him, and it was fascinating because it was all about the mathematics of music. I'd studied other methods earlier, but this was so enlightening because it showed you how to figure

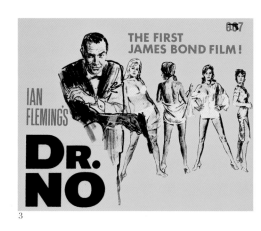

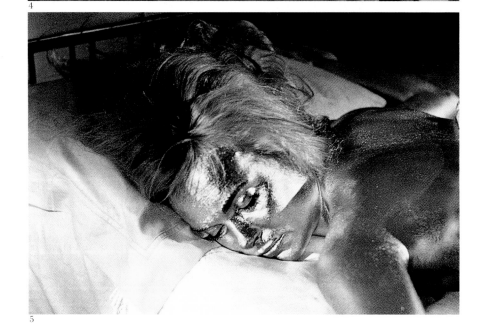

(1, 4, 5) The Bond style was defined in **Goldfinger** with Barry's theme and score, Ken Adams' sets and Robert Brownjohn's title sequences. For key scenes Barry incorporated hard, metallic sounds into the score: "of gold, the hardness of it". (2) John Barry with the Moviola in 1967. (3) Poster for **Dr No**. (6) Conducting the orchestra for **You Only Live Twice** in 1967. "In the Bond movies I used the theme dramatically throughout. Melody registers in the most fundamental way with audiences. I like to get a melody that will stand repetition so I'm not coming at it the same way every time." (7) **Diamonds are Forever**.

6

7

(1) John Barry conducting the music for **Mary Queen of Scots** in 1971. (2–4) **Midnight Cowboy**: "This was the first dramatic movie that used a lot of songs in the score and I totally structured the songs, including Nilsson's 'Everybody's Talking'."

FRESH COCONUTS 40¢

out why scales and harmonies are structured the way they are, purely through mathematical form. It clarified the whole of musical structure for me – he went into the 12-tone scale and all the rest of it – so you understood everything from a purely technical point of view.

At 19 I went into the army and joined the military band with the Green Howards. We were stationed in Cyprus, and I'd read in *Downbeat* magazine that Bill Russo, who was Stan Kenton's composer, had left the band and was giving a correspondence course from Chicago called 'Composition and Orchestration for the Jazz Orchestra'. I was a big Kenton fan, and so I used to go into Larnaca every week to buy dollars to send to Bill Russo so I could do the course. I had a hut on my own with a piano, so for the 16 months I was there I studied with Russo which was fantastic because there were no distractions. It was a very detailed course and he had about 20 students, but I think he used to devote a little extra time to me because I was the only European.

I'd gone into the army in the early '50s knowing all the band leaders like Ted Heath, Johnny Dankworth and Jack Parnell because they played my father's theatres, and so I thought that when I came out I'd start doing arrangements. But over the three years things had changed – the big bands were struggling; they were 16-piece bands and they were dying. Now it was skiffle groups in London – people like Bill Hayley and the Comets, Freddy Bell and the Bell Boys – the rock and roll thing had started in the States. Jack Parnell suggested I start a small, really commercial group because he knew I

didn't want to work for anybody else, so I formed the John Barry Seven with three local musicians and three I had been in the army with. We started by copying what was coming out of America. Essentially, we were all contemporary jazz fans. I bought the first bass guitar that an English group ever had – a Hoffner – and I had to wean Fred Kirk, the bass player, off the double bass and on to this thing. He learned it quickly and we had pretty immediate success. It was a very viable group – we were playing contemporary music; we could do a 20-minute spot of our own and accompany other acts. We toured with Paul Anka and then got a recording contract with EMI. During that time I met Adam Faith – we had a whole slew of big hits. He was picked by a producer called George Willoughby to do a movie called **Beat Girl** – a kind of English beatnik movie, pretty terrible but there was room for me to move. I'd always wanted to do film scores and it was difficult to get involved in, as it was dominated by classical composers like Muir Mathieson and Malcolm Arnold. At that time, 1959, there were no young composers coming up through the pop field. But it was just starting to change then.

I also did a lot of commercials, which was very lucrative and also educational – it taught you how to work to a brief, how to abbreviate, to cram something into a short space and be immediately effective. And through doing commercials I worked with directors like Karel Reisz and Dick Lester. In a movie like **The Knack**, for example, you can see how Dick Lester had learned that new style of quick cutting from his television work. So I was the only young person who was coming up through pop music at that time, but I also had the other elements in my musical training – the classical and the jazz. Later on, when I did **The Lion in Winter**, people said it was a new departure for me, but it wasn't – it was just my early training with Francis Jackson, the choral music I'd studied. And again, when I wrote a jazz club sequence for **The L-Shaped Room**, I was able to use this other part of my early training.

I was chosen to do the main title music for the first Bond film, **Dr No**, because I'd already had two or three instrumental hits. They were dissatisfied with what they already had, and wanted something quick. I worked on it over a weekend, booked the orchestra and we recorded it the following Wednesday morning. I hadn't seen the movie, or read an Ian Fleming book, but I knew the James Bond strip in *The Daily Mail*. I was given a timing of something like two minutes 20 seconds, and told they wanted a contemporary sound.

I think it still stands up, but when you listen to it you can see how it develops from my earlier work. The James Bond theme has the same rhythms as 'Bee's Knees', the signature tune of the John Barry Seven, and the opening of **Beat Girl**, which had a similar guitar riff which the orchestra then built on. The whole opening is like what I learned from Bill Russo – the Stan Kenton Brass; big, open, low trombones, and tight trumpet for that very explosive sound; then it's the guitar riff; then it breaks into a swing thing and that whole bridge, which is almost like a Dizzy Gillespie be-bop phrase. It was a really mixed bag of tricks. United Artists were delighted with it and wanted me to carry on with the series. I did the score for

From Russia with Love – Lionel Bart, who'd just had a big hit with **Oliver**, wrote the song, which I orchestrated and then used the theme occasionally throughout the movie. On **Goldfinger**, the next one along which came out in 1964, I told them I wanted to do everything this time. So I wrote the theme and then I called up Anthony Newley and Leslie Bricusse who wrote the lyrics and I asked Shirley Bassey to sing it. I hate the idea of just sticking a song at the beginning of a movie – I wanted to use the thematic music in the song dramatically throughout the movie. A lot of writers in the '30s would write a theme for a movie and repeat it throughout – perhaps not as expansively as I did, but this was the classical way of scoring movies. But my main themes were in the songs, and this was the Bond style.

For me, orchestration is part of the composition process, because when I'm writing I'm making mental notes about what the orchestration is going to be, so they're inseparable. In this way, you can use the orchestration in an unusual way for greater resonance. In **Goldfinger**, for example, I used the sound of finger cymbals – you hear it the first time you see Oddjob. I wanted the sound of metal, and finger cymbals are very small but they have a distinctive "ting" sound – it was the whole idea of metal, of gold and the hardness of it. You can hear this too in the use of brass at the beginning – the trombones and horns in the introduction to the song. In **Goldfinger**, everything came together – musically and also in terms of design. **Goldfinger** defined the mood and style for the whole series.

2

3

(1–3) **Midnight Cowboy:** The deliberately unsophisticated harmonica theme became a very big hit in America soon after the film opened: "The counter-melody is much more important than the melody, in that it's going nowhere – it's just this repetitive thing, like when you travel around New York and see the homeless and you see these people going nowhere. That's where the falling motif for John Voight's character comes from."

1

2

3

(1–3) **Out of Africa**: Barry succeeded in writing a highly memorable and melodic score for a film whose original screenplay had very little narrative. He involved himself deeply with the two main characters, producing a theme based primarily on their interaction with the landscape surrounding them: "I tried to put myself in their situation as a dramatist, so it is what they are seeing that the music has to reflect."

On **Midnight Cowboy**, we used an existing song, Harry Nilsson's 'Everybody's Talking', which set the mood for the whole film, but we re-recorded it to specific lengths and that's why it's so tight – it wasn't just fading in and fading out. All the other songs were written specifically for the film, we didn't just buy records and lay them in, which is what so often happens today. John Schlesinger, the director, was insistent that we shouldn't have any song in the movie that wasn't serving the overall vision, and this was a very astute observation. Once we started to plot the movie it became evident there was going to be a score, and so I wrote the harmonica theme in which the counter-melody is more important than the melody, giving a general repetitive feeling like going nowhere, to reflect the underbelly of New York. For the actual melody, I wanted something very unsophisticated that any guy sitting outside a gas station in Texas could play. We kept the instrumentation very simple – 12-string guitars, a rhythm section and the harmonica, so that the theme of 'Midnight Cowboy' in the score would fit into the musical language of the Nilsson song. I used other musical elements for the nightmare sequence flashbacks – futuristic elements, old Texan nursery rhymes – which I saw as a way of subconsciously describing what was going on in the picture – it helps you to focus in on Joe and the horror of his situation.

By contrast, for the music for the Florida sequence we wanted something happy and corny. I remembered a sergeant from the army who was always drunk and who played tenor saxophone really badly but thought he was terrific – he was the inspiration for this section. I used a Moog synthesizer just to make it a little off-key – it gives it a certain strangeness.

At the other end of the scale, **Out of Africa** called for a score which was lyrical, sweeping and romantic. The director, Sydney Pollack, stressed the importance of using the score to make an emotional connection with the audience – the danger would be to simply end up just using big music and playing the scenery. I used the same approach here as I did for **Dances with Wolves**; I picked two main themes and used them as a dramatist might, imagining what the character is seeing and thinking, and used the music to reflect this. In the opening shot, when Karen stands at the back of the train, there's an initial section which sets the mood and the mystery of the place – what Africa must have been like to those people at that time. Then Karen's theme comes in, and here it was a question of writing music which would be very melodic and memorable, with a strong emotional resonance which would position her firmly into the heart of the film. Sydney had warned me that the story had no real narrative – "it's just two people behaving". For this reason it was vital that the music should dramatise the characters' thoughts and emotions.

It was also important not to overscore. I wrote only 35 minutes of music for **Out of Africa** (compared with 90 minutes for **Dances with Wolves**). It seems like a big score because Sydney's direction was so specific and the structure firmly dictated where the music should go, but we loved the silences and the sounds of Africa – the animal sounds or the winds which seemed to reflect its vastness, the sound of fire when the farm burns – I didn't want to swamp any of that.

1

(1–2) **Out of Africa**: (1) John Barry re-recorded the safari scene. He had initially written it "big" to begin with, taking it down as Karen's journey progressed. Sydney Pollack was unhappy with the way he had shot it and asked Barry to reverse this: "He said, 'I want it to start small and become triumphant'." (2) "What struck me was the scale of Africa. The one thing that is essential in a good score is getting the scale of the scene right, the environment, the size, the look of it, the intimacy of it. That's a major part of composing for film." (right) John Barry at his piano.

2

In other places, I used the orchestration to reflect the wide open spaces of Africa. In the flying scene this is particularly important. I felt that for two people flying over this landscape in a small plane, the experience would be spiritual and not triumphant. I think it would have been a sense of mystery, an air of grandeur that was beyond comprehension, and so I used the voices here, and the images on screen – when the plane swoops down and all the birds start to fly – seemed to reinforce this theme. In terms of orchestration, this was a very classical piece of work, with a very strong, falling melody in the violas – it wasn't highly stylised at all.

In working with the director, it's important that you should be able to surprise them – you shouldn't just try to do what they want and no more. This is why I like working with directors like Sydney Pollack or John Schlesinger. Good directors will leap on a surprise and see that you have added something fresh and valuable; there are always areas where a score can vastly help in the telling of the story. The most important thing is to find your own voice as a film composer – it's orchestration, but it's also your own harmonic and melodic voice. Having done that, you can work on contrasting scores, whether it's a Bond movie or **Midnight Cowboy** or **Out of Africa**; they're all vastly different subjects, period, theme and style, but the music will have a certain characteristic voice which always comes through – your own musical DNA.

biography

Born in Argentina in 1932, Lalo Schifrin studied at the Paris Conservatoire and was later talent-spotted playing jazz by Dizzy Gillespie. A move to the U.S. led to a contract with Verve Records, a division of MGM. His first film score was composed in Argentina for **El Jefe/The Chief** (1957), and, having settled in Hollywood in 1964, he went on to write music for films such as **The Cincinnati Kid** (1965, Norman

lalo schifrin

Jewison); **The President's Analyst** (1967, Theodore J. Flicker); **Cool Hand Luke** (1967, Stuart Rosenburg); and **Bullitt** (1968, Peter Yates). During the 1970s, he wrote a wide range of scores including **Kelly's Heroes** (1970, Brian G. Hutton); **The Beguiled** (1970) and **Dirty Harry** (1971), both directed by Don Siegel; **Enter the Dragon** (1973, Robert Clouse) and **Rollercoaster** (1977, James Goldstone). He has since worked with directors such as Clint Eastwood (**Sudden Impact**, 1983) and Sam Peckinpah (**The Osterman Weekend**, 1983). In more recent years Schifrin has written scores for **Tango** (1998, Carlos Saura) and **Rush Hour** (1998, Brett Ratner). He has also written music for the concert hall, including a series, 'Jazz Meets the Symphony' and an oratorio, 'The Rise and Fall of the Third Reich'. The characteristic "Schifrin sound" is a blend of jazz and contemporary music with a seemingly limitless ability to create melodies that stay with an audience long after the credits have finished rolling.

interview

I'd say I had a very classical musical education. My father was concert master of the Buenos Aires Philharmonic Orchestra for 35 years. I went to all the rehearsals and I took piano lessons from the father of Daniel Barenboim. When I was about seven years old, I started to get interested in music in movies, along with some class mates. We went to see many movies, and after one particular horror film I arrived at the conclusion that, without the music, it wouldn't have been so frightening. When I was old enough, I would go four or five times a week on my own just to see the same movie because you couldn't buy soundtracks then. I went to see **Alexander Nevsky** 14 times because of Prokofiev's score.

I began to wake up to the music of the 20th century. I was attending a masterclass at the National Conservatory of Music and my teacher was Juan Carlos Paz, who had been a pupil of Schoenberg in Vienna before the war. He introduced me to the music of Boulez and together we analysed the score of 'Le

(1) Lalo Schifrin playing the piano.
(2–3) **Hell in the Pacific**: "Sometimes I'll integrate sound effects as in **Hell in the Pacific** where there's a cut which starts with the sound of a cicada. Then I took two piccolos at the same pitch and continued the idea: the audience didn't know where the sound effect ended and the music started."

Marteau sans mâitre'. He advised me to apply for a scholarship to the Paris Conservatoire: I passed the examination and was accepted into the classes of Olivier Messiaen. Parallel to all this, I had a serious interest in jazz. I don't believe you can actually "learn" jazz in an academic sense, but I would listen to pianists like Art Tatum and Thelonious Monk on 78s and slow them down to 33 so that I could copy the parts as their lines were so fast. Then, of course, I tried to develop my own style as a jazz musician.

When I went to Paris I led a double life. I decided I needed to have my own apartment as the City University dorms were terrible, so I started to play jazz for a living in the evening. When Messiaen found out that I was a jazz musician, he practically stopped talking to me. He thought it was rhythmically boring – he didn't understand that jazz has its own dynamics, its own articulation in terms of rhythm. When I returned to Argentina at the age of 22, I was given the opportunity to have my own Big Band. The new Director of State Television and Radio loved jazz, and he'd heard about me and asked me to write all the arrangements for a band he'd established. My next lucky break was when Dizzy Gillespie visited Buenos Aires with his All Star band, and there was a reception for him where I played the piano with my band. He heard me and asked if I wrote the arrangements. When I told him I had, he asked me if I would like to go to the U.S. I thought he was kidding but he wasn't. It took me nearly two years to get to the States as an immigrant, during which time I did my first movie in Argentina, **The Chief**, which was a kind of allegory of the Peron era. I used some jazz

instrumentation for that movie, though I wouldn't call it a jazz score. They gave me the Argentinean equivalent of an Academy Award for it, but by that time I was already in the U.S. I'd become the in-house arranger for Verve Records, working with artists like Ella Fitzgerald, Count Basie, Stan Getz, Sarah Vaughan and, of course, Dizzy Gillespie.

It was through MGM that I went to Hollywood. My first major film was **The Cincinnati Kid**, and I was lucky enough to work with a good director, Norman Jewison. I felt that the film-making process was a collaboration, like playing in a band, the leader being the director. But a director has an advantage over a composer, which is that he's been involved in a movie from the very inception, so he knows the piece inside out and he knows all the scenes where, for instance, the actors aren't giving him quite what he wants, and he might just need some music to help lift a scene. This happened occasionally in **The Cincinnati Kid**, but there are also some interesting scenes where the music creates a counterpoint – a parallel motion – to the visuals. There's quite a brutal scene of a cock-fight, where the music is almost comic. I remember using a banjo and a fiddle like they do in country music, but when the cocks get together – if you listen closely – I do brass clusters, so it becomes something a little like Charles Ives. I had some percussion in there as well, all ignoring each other. I'm very satisfied with that particular music – its comedy underlined the cruelty of the scene.

I used the same technique in **Rollercoaster**. (There's a classic example of this audio-visual counterpoint in

5

6

(3–7) **The Cincinnati Kid**: This was Schifrin's first major feature score. (3) This manuscript for 'Mr Slade' is from the conductor's score; note the short score orchestration. Schifrin's score often runs contrary to the action. (1–2, 4) This type of juxtaposition is something he particularly admired in the fairground scene of Hitchcock's **Strangers on a Train** and he subsequently used it to effect in his score for **Rollercoaster** and for the brutal cock-fight in **The Cincinnati Kid** with comic banjo and fiddle music. (5–6) "There was a lot of tension during the poker games where there was no jazz at all, but instead there was the influence of Messiaen."

7

Hitchcock's **Strangers on a Train**, where the murder takes place in an amusement park and as this happens you hear the merry-go-round predominantly on the soundtrack.) Another scene I think works well is when Edward G. holds up the joker in the final card scene. The brass cluster there was structured by following the camera cutting between all the faces of the people at the table. It's very simple – it has to do with the psychology of perception, as the audience imagines what the actors must be thinking, trying to guess which card it is. The music here had an important function – it had to bind the scene together and build tension – but if I had to do it again now, I'd probably do it a completely different way!

It's very important to decide where music starts and music ends. I like to catch the common denominator of a scene, instead of catching everything like in a cartoon. In movies, it's more interesting to capture the general atmosphere of a scene once in a while, with an accent of some kind. I think silence can be very effective – I don't think it's necessary to "fill" a movie with music wall-to-wall, which is a tendency nowadays.

For instance, in **Bullitt**, the main thing for me was to avoid showing too early that Robert Vaughn was the villain. I could have done that by putting all his scenes to music, but that would have given away the plot. Also, I think the director, Peter Yates, establishes characters and relationships in a very subtle way. Very early on in the movie he wanted to convey the love affair between Steve McQueen and Jacqueline Bisset, and instead of doing a love scene, he cuts to a bar away from all the police problems and investigations, and there's a jazz

trio playing. The interesting thing about that scene is that he does it all without them saying a word, he just cuts from their faces to the jazz trio and back again, and you understand what the relationship is.

Going back to the absence of music, people always tell me what great music I wrote for the car chase, but I didn't. I wrote four minutes before the chase, where the villains are playing cat-and-mouse with McQueen, and I built the tension when McQueen shifted gears, and then the chase began. I told them the orchestration had to be done with sound effects. The important thing was that there were two different cars and each of them had a different sound: we had to use that so the audience could identify which car was which – you couldn't always tell just from the image on screen. Too much music would have made the film muddy. It would have been out of proportion to come on with a big, pompous theme when everything else is so understated, so sometimes there's just rhythmic things happening. Bullitt is, after all, a very cool guy and McQueen inspired me to want to reflect this.

Again, early on in **Dirty Harry** I used rhythm rather than big themes – the tabla was perfect here, because it's subtle and it doesn't have an obvious pulse like congas or bongos. The opening sequence is a combination of bells, harp, clusters and voices. When Don Siegel, the director, told me about the character of Scorpio, the killer, I immediately decided I was going to use voices for him. Maybe it was because of the Charles Manson thing, when they said they were hearing voices – I don't know, I didn't do it consciously. I decided to

1

2

3

(1–3) **Tango**: The music for this film shows Schifrin's versatility, a composer equally at home with a jazz or classical score. "This film was the only time I thought about the music first, but in all the other films I've done the music has come afterwards, and the influence, the texture, the photography, the way the actors act – that influences me a lot."

film music

2

1

(1–4) **Bullitt**: (1–2) The car chase is one of the most famous action scenes of film history: "Many people have said that the music I wrote for the chase is fantastic, but I didn't write any music for this scene – I wrote four minutes before the chase, where the villians are playing cat-and-mouse in the traffic, and then I build and build the tension. Then when Steve McQueen shifts the gear, bang, they are going." (3) Opening page of Schifrin's 'Main Title' conductor score. The drum part (bottom stave) is completely notated. Note big-band type brass stabs in bar eight. This cool, laid-back music with a hint of dissonance infuses the film with much of its style and excitement.

(1–3) **Dirty Harry**: "There are three traditions with thrillers: the French tradition is psychology, the British tradition is suspense, and the American tradition is action." For **Dirty Harry** Schifrin provided the rhythm with tablas: "I used these instead of the conga drums or the bongos as I needed to establish a pulse. Then you build and build and build... into silence." (right) Lalo Schifrin with Dizzy Gillespie.

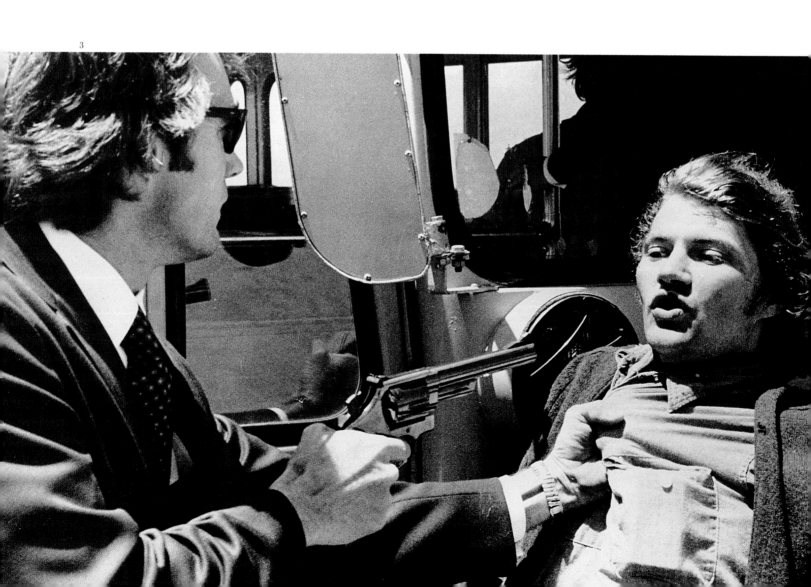

have the voices at an unusual interval, not exactly unpleasant, but enough to build the tension so that, when the character is running, there are three or four voices together and the music seems to become hysterical. I would say the theme for the cool Dirty Harry character is very masculine, with its doubling up of the bass riff with cellos. He's a guy who's very sure of himself – despite the fact that he doesn't have a clue who the killer is, he knows his business. There's pathos in there too, like with the electric piano motif, which I introduce when they discover the girl. It comes three or four times in the film, and at the end when he throws away his badge.

People talk about the so-called "Lalo Schifrin sound" and its combination of jazz with contemporary music, and sometimes they expect a certain thing, that you can repeat a score. After **Dirty Harry**, I was asked to do another crime thriller but I just couldn't do it – I had to let some time go by. This has happened on a few occasions.

I like to have control over my music and, even though there's a jazz feel, I don't allow improvisation; I score everything. I always like to conduct my work and I do all my own orchestrating, although I have taken advice occasionally. For instance, an orchestrator advised me to reinforce the bassline with bassoons – he was very aware of the frequencies of bass instruments and that they can cause a rumble. This was useful advice, and I would say that now my bass writing is more transparent. It's also a good thing to make time to attend the dubbing process – I was given this advice by Henry Mancini and I try to follow it to protect my work, to make sure the sound, the dialogue and also the music are mixed properly in the finished film.

I feel that in my work I've embraced the two great art forms of the 20th century – jazz and film. This still seems incredible to me because, when I began, you couldn't study those subjects as you can now – I just arrived there by intuition.

biography

Born in London in 1944, Michael Nyman studied composition with Alan Bush at The Royal Academy Of Music and musicology with Thurston Dart at King's College, London. As a music critic he wrote for *The Listener*, *New Statesman*, and *The Spectator*. He coined the term "minimalism" as a description of music in October 1978. In 1976 he formed The Michael Nyman Band which has performed many of his

michael nyman

concert works and film scores. As a composer he's written four String Quartets, two Operas, five Concerti and many other works. Nyman's reached his largest audience as a film composer, most famously for Peter Greenaway, with whom he collaborated on 11 movies between 1976 and 1991. Most spectacular has been the success of the soundtrack album for Jane Campion's **The Piano**; it has sold three million copies, establishing Nyman as the best-selling living British classical composer. He has collaborated with Peter Greenaway on **1–100** (1978); **The Draughtsman's Contract** (1982); **A Zed & Two Noughts** (1985); **Drowning by Numbers** (1988); **The Cook, the Thief, His Wife and Her Lover** (1989) and **Prospero's Books** (1991). He has written scores for numerous other directors: Robert Young (**Keep it Up Downstairs**, 1976); Patrice Leconte (**Monsieur Hire**, 1989; **The Hairdresser's Husband**, 1990); Jane Campion (**The Piano**, 1993), Andrew Niccol (**Gattaca**, 1997) and Neil Jordan (**The End Of The Affair**, 1999).

interview

I can remember being conscious of soundtracks as a child – I remember going to see a film called **Where No Vultures Fly**, and noticing it had a soundtrack by English composer Alan Rawsthorne. Then I suppose my all-time favourite as a kid was **The Big Country** score by Jerome Moross, who I'd never heard of. As a child there was absolutely no music in my house, apart from what was on the radio and television; but when I changed primary schools in 1952 I was kind of "discovered" by the music teacher. From the age of seven he gave me a broad and intensive musical education. I was at The Royal Academy Of Music from 1961 to 1963. Then I went into musicology and became a music critic on *The Spectator*. Around my time at the Academy I met Peter Greenaway. He was working at the British Film Institute and lived in this rambling house where he'd actually created a cinema in the back room. He used to borrow films and run them on Friday and Saturday nights – experimental films by people like Eisenstein and Godard. It was a fantastic

1

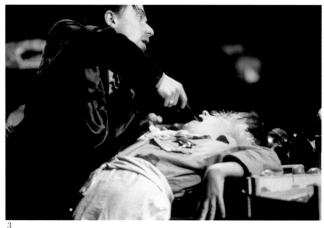

(1–3) **The Cook, the Thief, His Wife and Her Lover**: (1) Nyman's manuscript for 'Memorial'. Peter Greenaway wanted a "slow, processional, menacing, dark, repetitive piece". Nyman played him a cassette of 'Memorial' which he had written four years earlier, and Greenaway choreographed the whole procession sequence to that recording: "The tape was the first performance of that piece – it was very shaky and kept changing tempos. When I re-recorded it for the film I was listening on headphones to the original, trying to duplicate the waywardness of this performance."

education for me. My film composition career actually started much later after two radically different experiences in 1976. Greenaway asked me to write the soundtrack for a film called **1–100**, for which I wrote highly intellectualised music. Simultaneously I did a mainstream EMI film called **Keep it Up Downstairs**, a British romp which involved me making arrangements of Edwardian salon music. I certainly had no idea which way my career would go – even if there was going to be a career.

I took the Greenaway route because we enjoyed working together. We established a method of working which continued for another 15 years. While I was writing the music Peter would be shooting and editing the film. I'd give him the music, and he would say, "oh yes, this piece fits much better at the end, instead of at the beginning". So the music created an editing rhythm. The traditional Hollywood way is to do the final edit, list the cues then ask for the music. But this way round it meant I wasn't just a dummy who slotted music in.

In **The Draughtsman's Contract** Greenaway wanted the music to act as a locating device. The "draughtsman" makes 12 drawings from different viewpoints, and each requires its own piece of music which the audience can identify. These 12 pieces, like the drawing process, grow and develop in six stages. The concepts of **The Draughtsman's Contract** were 1980s', but being set at the end of the 17th century, it had to have a 17th-century content. Since we were dealing with drawings, frames, and something that was fixed, it seemed logical to use ground basses – because one of the attractions

of that form is a sense of being locked into the musical frame. And though the ground bass is a 17th-century concept, it's also timeless. Purcell was the best English composer of that era and as a musicologist I'd studied his music and his use of ground basses. So I went back to The University of London Music Library and just picked out the bits that really appealed to me. For the first drawing, I built music from the ground upwards: the bass part, then a bit more detail, and more again, until the sixth version, which was to represent the finished drawing. But Peter heard this sixth version and thought, "it's amazing, we have to start the film with this". So, as they're tramping across the fields with all the drawing paraphernalia in the heavy mist, instead of rather hesitant opening music you get this great fanfare which I'd intended to represent the completed drawing in all its glory. Another time, I used the bass as a melody and overlaid multiple cascading harpsichord arpeggios. Greenaway used this music to accompany the drawings being burned. I think that's a fantastic representation of burning, yet it was totally unintentional. If he'd asked me to represent fire musically I would have said, "I can't do it", because I hate doing those descriptive things.

In most of the films I've done for Greenaway there's a sense in which the music grows and develops maybe more than the film does. Music is unexplainable, even the composer is never sure what it's going to sound like until the music is laid to the picture – and how the scene is going to feel with the addition of this totally alien art form. And yet usually it's just something that's added on at the end of the film-making

michael nyman

(1–5) **The Hairdresser's Husband**:
The bizarre tale of the film (a young
boy falls in love with his hairdresser
and attempts to recapture this love in
adult life by marrying a different
hairdresser) unfolds through a series
of character revelations and bizarre
flashbacks, and is well explored by
Nyman's minimalist score.

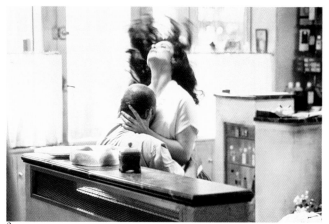

5

michael nyman

3

4

process. The director, having spent six months editing may have just six days to put the music on. So it actually puts the composer in a very unfair position; sometimes brilliant things can come out of it, sometimes they don't.

Jane Campion is, like Greenaway, a film-maker who creates that kind of visual emotional world, and she recognised in me the ability to create a self-contained independent world in music for **The Piano**. I didn't realise how important that would be until I saw the film. The major problem with **The Piano** was creating its musical language; there were two conflicting elements; it had to be mid-19th century but also my own voice. I was writing the music that Holly Hunter plays even before the film was shot. I met her in New York and we went to the Steinway Showroom where she played her party pieces. She's really quite a good pianist so that encouraged me. I was fearful that the music might be limited by her technique, as the piano music is a crucial part not only of the film's sound world but of the expression of Ada's character. Campion and I went through the script and blocked out where the piano pieces would be. I spent a month agonising over how I should write this music. I think the solution to the problem was realising that if Hunter's character, Ada, had spoken, she would have used her own words – so she had to be a composer. Once I'd decided that, things became easier; she could write any kind of music and since she wasn't a trained composer she could write music that sounded like 1990s' minimalist music, or she could take a theme that she might have heard locally in Scotland and treat it like one of Mendelssohn's 'Songs Without Words'. For some of the music

I sampled Chopin, just little segments repeated from Chopin's 'Mazurkas' and I based a lot of the music on Scottish folk music, which is timeless. Campion edited to a temp track of Ada's music, and so made decisions about the film – for the terrifying sequence where Sam Neill chases Holly and eventually cuts off her finger, Campion used the main theme. There's no way I would have had the nerve to do it, it just wouldn't have occurred to me. But it works extremely well.

When it came to **Gattaca**, Andrew Niccol, the director, again recognised this ability to conjure up a self-contained musical world. **Gattaca**'s a film with a European attitude made with Hollywood money. Composing for a Hollywood movie is very different to a European art movie. For one thing the support system in Hollywood is overwhelming – you've got copyists, a music editor – for every film I did before **Gattaca** I had to do everything myself. Niccol knew exactly what kind of soundtrack he wanted. In fact, when I told him I don't do futuristic sci-fi music, bleeps and blobs, he said that's not what he wanted. His temp track was Górecki's 'Third Symphony', plus a few bits of Philip Glass. If there's a really good temp track on a movie you actually don't need to look at the film, and **Gattaca** was like that. Niccol invited me to write whatever music I wanted to – he said, "we don't need to synchronise with anything, we'll just have the music flowing over the sequences". From that I could tell Niccol was very sophisticated musically. I also knew I had to take the Górecki as a starting point but deviate from it radically.

I took the instrumentation directly from his 'Third Symphony',

1

3

2

(1–2) **Drowning by Numbers**: Nyman based his score on the slow movement of Mozart's 'Sinfonia Concertante', and then developed a set of variations as deconstructions which match the mood of the sumptuous images, making this possibly his most accessible Greenaway score: "I re-recorded the Mozart because we couldn't afford to pay for the rights of the recording we'd used. Recreating the tempo changes was the most difficult thing I've ever had to do." (3) Nyman at Abbey Road studios in 1991.

(1–7) **The Piano**: "I sat down to write in my house, a building site at the time, with the synthesizer resting on a workbench – the first time I had composed not on a piano. So one of my most sensitive scores was written on an instrument with no sensitivity whatsoever." Jane Campion rejected some of the score, preferring Nyman's temp track of pre-cropped pieces. "Campion's since admitted she was over-cautious with the music." (5–6) Two pages of Michael Nyman's manuscript and score for **The Piano**.

7

4

michael nyman

5

6

1

2

3

4

5   6

(1–7) **Gattaca**: "I told Andrew Niccols, 'I don't do futuristic sci-fi music, I don't do bleeps and blobs' and he said, 'Fine, that's not what I want'. He wanted me to use Górecki's 'Third Symphony' as a starting point." (3–4) Two pages from Nyman's manuscript score for **Gattaca**. The figures at the top refer to the "Reel" number. A film is divided into five Reels, so IMI refers to Reel I, Music cue I. The first page contains sketches for various musical ideas, complete with timing calculations, while page two is Nyman's final orchestral score.

7

(1, 3–4) **The Draughtsman's Contract**: (1) The score for Nyman's music for 'Drawing'. Note the top stave is the ground bass part taken from music by 17th-century English composer, Henry Purcell; it repeats over and over, above which new music is added. "I returned to the same Purcell Society volumes that I'd looked at when I was a student and just picked out the bits that really appealed to me." (2) Nyman playing the piano while reading the paper.

but achieving the same effect was more to do with pace and style – you don't hear Górecki as a background.

Niccol was absolutely drivingly meticulous, not only as to what music he wanted but in his approach to rewrites. One day he would say, "yes, I like 90 per cent of this score", and then I would get a fax saying, "well, this cue doesn't work, this one doesn't work, this one doesn't work", so I'd end up rewriting 50 per cent again. But I respect directors differently according to how musically sussed they are, and Niccol was sharp – I knew that if he didn't think something worked then it didn't work. So I didn't mind rewriting it. Even three or four days before the recording session I was doing rewrites. Because Niccol sort of hovered over me, literally and metaphorically, I did something I'd never done before which was a synthesizer demo of the whole score to make it sound as much like the final orchestral version as possible. Normally I never do synthesizer demos because they take too much time and I think they sound terrible. I think one of the best things I've written is the end music of **Gattaca**. It's got this forward-looking grandeur but also a sense of tragedy. Two things happen simultaneously; Ethan Hawke leaves in a spaceship, fulfilling his dream, and Jude Law is left behind and immolates himself. Originally that sequence was much more complex so I wrote a piece which kept changing as it cut from the spaceship to the furnace. Then very late in the day I got a new edit, much smoother. Straight off I wrote the theme you hear, based on the harmonies of the three earlier swimming sequences. When there are situations in a film that are paralleled I like to have variations of the same music.

I think producers and music supervisors often don't understand my music, and if they do they give me totally unsuitable scripts. I don't write conventional film music. I suppose it has to do with the sound I make and the way my music moves – it doesn't just fall into that easy motion that other film music does. That's because I'm an experimental composer; that's just how it comes out naturally. Yes, people hire me, but sometimes they don't know what they're getting and sometimes, as with Campion and Niccol, they've asked me to do things that even I didn't know I could do.

biography

Born in 1949, Gabriel Yared was passionately fond of music from an early age and in 1970 he decided to abandon his law studies to devote himself to it. He made his professional debut in Brazil, working with Elis Regina and Ivan Lins. He moved to Paris in 1972, where he composed and orchestrated songs for French stars such as Charles Aznavour and Sylvie Vartan, and in 1980 began to collaborate with the director

gabriel yared

Jean-Luc Godard, to produce his first film score for **Sauve Qui Peut, La Vie** (1980). **Betty Blue** (1986), with the director Jean-Jacques Beineix, brought him international acclaim. They also collaborated on **Moon in the Gutter** (1983) and **IP5** (1991). He worked with Robert Altman on **Beyond Therapy** (1987) and **Vincent & Theo** (1990). His other films include **Hanna K** (1984, Costa-Gavras); **Camille Claudel** (1988, Bruno Nuytten); **The Lover** (1991, Jean-Jacques Annaud); **Map of the Human Heart** (1992, Vincent Ward); **Wings of Courage** (1994, Jean-Jacques Annaud); **City of Angels** (1998, Brad Silberling) and **Message in a Bottle** (Luis Mandoki, 1999). He won an Oscar and a Golden Globe Award for **The English Patient** (1996, Anthony Minghella) and worked with him again on the music for **The Talented Mr Ripley** (1999).

interview

I didn't have a musical background, except for one hour a week of piano lessons at boarding school. I was given an 'Invention' by Bach, and instead of learning it I began to decipher it so that music became the first language for me, not French or English. It was very easy for me to read music when I was ten years old, and all the things I've learned are from reading music. Later I went to Brazil for The Festival of Song in Rio de Janeiro. I stayed in Brazil with a small band which played my compositions. At the time I was very influenced by The Beatles, Randy Newman and Stevie Wonder. Then I left Brazil to return to Lebanon, and on the way back I came through Paris. I ended up staying here. I worked as an orchestrator for French pop singers like Johnny Hallyday and Françoise Hardy, whose husband, Jacques Dutronc, was acting with Jean-Luc Godard. I didn't know this director's work, in fact I didn't know anything about movies. But I met him, and began to work with him, and for the first time someone was asking me to read a script – there was

1

3

2

Gabriel YARED

5

(1–5) **Betty Blue**: The original score was recorded on a small budget so many of the sounds were played on synthesizers. But the music has been so successful that Yared has made a 'Betty Blue Suite' for Orchestra. (2) Part of the opening section where the main theme is played on the First Violins marked "cantabile" ("as if sung"). This is a good example of Yared's "simple theme with elegant harmony". Note the piano part above the harp's for Yared to play in concert.

nothing visual, no pictures, no cuts, no frames – just the script. I told him I didn't know anything about making music for a movie. He said, "don't worry, just use your imagination". He told me to compose my music and he would adapt it to the images. At the time, I only had one keyboard – an old analogue synthesizer – and I worked with a programmer on this. Godard came to the studio and took all this stuff away with him to edit with the rest of the film. I was very surprised and pleased with the result – **Sauve Qui Peut, La Vie**. For the first time, I realised how powerful music could be when it was combined with pictures. This was my first experience in making music for film and everything had come from my conversation with the director Godard and from reading the script, which – after 13 years now – still seems to me to be the best approach. This is the way I've done all my work – **Betty Blue, The English Patient** – it's music composed before the picture.

I always tell my agent to ask the director when he's casting his actors and choosing the location to "cast" me. I don't want to come in on a movie which is already shot. I want to be involved. I can't work any other way – to present me with the picture and ask me to do "spotting" would be completely barbaric. After my conversations with the director and reading the script, I try to create a theme for one or two characters. I start making my demo, and give this to the director. Usually they play it on the set, to the actors, the cinematographer – so everyone comes to know the music as the film is being made. This was the process we used on **Betty Blue**. Jean-Jacques Beineix, the director, said he had

found a beautiful story in a novel by Philippe Djian. I read it, and he suggested we do something very intimate musically. I felt exactly the same. I annotated the script with musical interventions and began playing with my DX7 synthesizer, working on a few themes. Then Jean-Jacques Beineix brought the actors round to my place so that we could create a duet between Béatrice Dalle and Jean-Hugues Anglade. Béatrice said she could only play piano with one finger but Jean-Hugues was learning Debussy ('Doctor Gradus ad Parnassum') so I created a synthesis of their two approaches and this became a crucial element in the film. Once again, this could only have happened through meeting the people involved and talking it over. The themes and melodies in the film are very simple. There's only one sax player, one guitarist and one percussionist – all the rest is synths, except for some accordion which I play. The music speaks to you because the harmonies are elegant; it's the kind of music that would please musicians as well as the untrained listener. Jean-Jacques Beineix and I decided not to push the music in a dramatic way, but to simply use it like a point of view. For instance, as Betty becomes more mad, we didn't want to create melodramatic music. There's only one slight suggestion of this, where I use a piano with samples and there's a subliminal vibration. I'm particularly proud of the main saxophone theme, as it's a homage to the Brazilian period of my life. For me, **Betty Blue** was the best marriage between music and picture.

For **Vincent & Theo**, which started out as a film for television, Robert Altman showed me the script and then I

gabriel yared

(1–4) **Vincent & Theo**: (1–2) Yared wrote the music before seeing the film. Although much of the score is synthesised you can see from the short score manuscript that Yared notated everything. Note that the top three parts of this cue are all for piano. (5) Yared's inspiration: 'Bedroom at Arles' (1888), by Vincent Van Gogh. "I don't trust my ear. I trust much more my eyes on paper."

1

(1–8) **Vincent & Theo**: (2, 6) "My work came much more dramatically from Van Gogh's paintings, particularly 'Sunflowers', (1887) and 'Starry Night', (1888), than from the film itself." (3–4) In this music cue the texture is much more dense and chromatic. Notice how the instrumentation is more colourful: cellos, bass clarinet, strings, flutes and, on the bottom stave, synth effects. Notice also at the top of the score page that the same cue has different numbering for the film and television versions.

2

5

6

7

8

worked out some themes. Once again, I didn't write my music to the picture, I began with one image, which became very important for me – Van Gogh's painting, 'The Sunflowers' (1887). Altman said he wanted music that was both haunting and had a destructive element in it. 'The Sunflowers' became a leitmotif for me and I drew on it for inspiration for the Vincent theme. For certain scenes Altman wanted sophisticated instrumentation, perhaps influenced by jazz or gypsy music, using violin and accordion – nothing vulgar. For the title sequence I had to try to match the vision of both Van Gogh and Robert Altman, creating a multi-layered effect with synths and other instruments introducing harsh stabbing sounds – it was music that came straight from the heart. I wanted the music to be bold enough to be a very good representation of Van Gogh's paintings. I had a book of the paintings and I used different ones to inspire the music for different scenes. For the scene when Vincent goes to Provence, I had another image in mind – the painting, 'La Nuit Étoilée' ('Starry Night') (1888). I looked at this obsessively and the music seemed to come from it. I also used the painting of his room – the small room with a chair – and I felt this would "sound" completely awkward, like Mozart mixed with a Berg or a Bartók line, which would be something very bizarre.

Although a lot of the music is electronic, the whole thing is scored together with the traditional instrumentation of the violin and accordion. That way I can build up a counterpoint. When you're writing, you can go much deeper into the creative process than by just playing piano or synth, because what you play on the piano is the only part you can hear, whereas in writing I try to develop the theme as a whole.

For me, orchestration is the number one preoccupation, and until **The English Patient**, I did all my own orchestration. I now have an orchestrator who works with me, but I give him everything on my Vision MIDI file – that is, every instrument separately annotated so there's nothing to create and nothing to add harmonically. I have a small home studio, with a mixing desk, two Emulators, a Canvas, a Kurzweil (which I'm very attached to) and my computer. I begin by improvising with all these elements and when I've finished I then take out my pen and start working on the development. I have to do this because I don't trust my ear, I trust much more my eyes on paper.

Anthony Minghella, who directed and wrote the screenplay for **The English Patient**, originally wanted to be a composer and a musician. He has a wonderful ear and a very eclectic interest in all music. When he writes, he has a vision of how the music could be with the scenes; in fact, I suspect he writes while listening to music because in his scripts almost all the source music is mentioned. It's so interesting to work with this kind of director – a real soul mate. It was his idea to use Márta Sebestyén singing a Turkish/Bulgarian folk song in Hungarian, and it was also his idea for Hannah, Juliette Binoche's character, to play the 'Goldberg Variations' on the piano. I love it when it's this melting pot, because I feel there are all these different elements in me – there's my multi-cultural background in Lebanon, Brazil, Europe; my love of

(1–3) **The English Patient**: "One of the reasons I started the music with a cor anglais, beginning the melody in a minor key and then going into this very Slavic/Arabic harmonic combination, was to evoke a sense of spaciousness, of the desert." Yared composed the music as a response to the script, before any shooting took place: "I always want to be involved in the picture." (3) Yared in a recording session.

1

2

(1–3) **The English Patient**: "In this film, I joined together the elegance of classisism, the writing of Bach and deep-rooted folk forms. As I originate from so many different cultures, the project really illustrated who I was." Director Anthony Minghella made Yared rewrite the "swinging in the church scene" several times. He was keen to maximise the swinging, lifting feel of the music. (3) In the manuscript note the interlocking, lilting string pizzicato figures in the bass and viola parts and the celeste part doubling the violas.

Slavic music, classical music, black music; my interest in Bach. For this reason, I felt that **The English Patient** was the best project to express who I am musically.

Anthony felt that I was the person who could achieve a sort of unity of all these elements. For instance, at the end, when the English patient is dying and Juliette Binoche is close to him, the music that was used during the shooting – and up until two weeks before they cut the negative – was Bach's 'Goldberg Variations'. But Anthony wanted me to expand on the Bach theme and create something new which completely matched the mood of the scene. I had to make the music fit the same tempo and geography, but never the same key or the same musical identity as Bach. It was the most terrible thing to ask a composer to do – to try and match Bach!

I tried to get the music to reflect the sense of space in the desert by starting with a cor anglais in a minor key, and then developing into a Slav/Arabian harmony. I did this before any shooting began. Anthony felt the same as me, that we would get much more as we went on during the process of making the film. The music in **The English Patient** is much more complicated thematically than, say, **Betty Blue**, because each theme is borrowing from previous ones and developing into a new one – the story itself is like that, with all those flashbacks. It made me try to find a relationship between every theme, but by suggesting rather than being too obvious. In the scene when Hannah swings in the church as she looks at the wall paintings, Anthony kept stressing that he wanted the music to suggest this lifting, swinging notion, and in the end we used the same theme that I did on the piano solo, 'The Convento di Sant' Anna', with pizzicato strings – harp and mandolins – closer to Vivaldi than the Neapolitan mandolin.

Music for me is a great spirit that I have to protect and respect. I've always loved music so much and I gave so much to her that she gives to me in return. I sit at the piano and play and themes come. I'm very lucky, and I feel if I don't maintain my respect for music then one day she will leave me. I spend all my time loving music, and if I have time to spare the only thing I do is read – some Bartók, some Byrd, some Stravinsky... I don't feel I'm a great composer or anything, I'm just a lucky person who loves music and whom music loves.

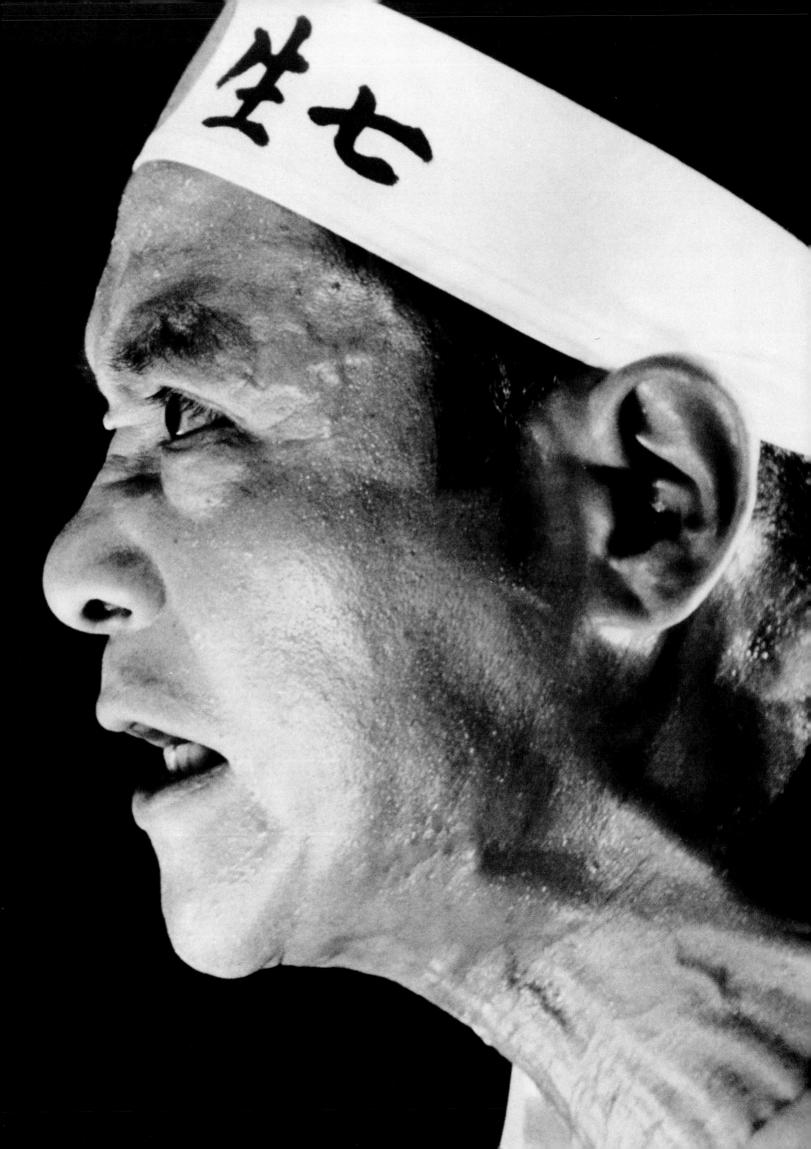

biography

Philip Glass was born in 1937. He studied at the Peabody Conservatory in Baltimore, the University of Chicago and the Juilliard School of Music in New York, as well as winning a Fulbright scholarship to study with Nadia Boulanger in Paris. From the age of 28 to 35 he continued his own course of learning in music and Eastern philosophy with Ravi Shankar, the sitar virtuoso. Glass has worked in most musical forms

philip glass

from chamber work to opera and his musical language has always excelled in being both innovative and accessible. He has collaborated very closely with director Godfrey Reggio on both **Koyaanisqatsi** (1983) and **Powaqqatsi** (1988), and worked at length with Martin Scorsese on **Kundun** (1997). Other films he has composed for include the documentaries **Mark Di Suvero** (1977, François De Menil) and **The Thin Blue Line** (1988, Errol Morris); **Mishima** (1985, Paul Schrader); **Hamburger Hill** (1987, John Irvin); **The Secret Agent** (1996, Christopher Hampton); and **The Truman Show** (1997, Peter Weir). Glass has recently written new scores for three of director Jean Cocteau's classic films: **La Belle et la Bête** (1946), **Les Enfants terribles** (1948) and **Orphée** (1949), as well as a score for Tod Browning's **Dracula** (1931).

interview

I came to film very late, really through the side door. My first film, by Barbara Rose, was in 1977, about the sculptor Mark Di Suvero. Basically I wrote music for the sculpture. It wasn't really a film score but it was a wonderful compilation of image and music. The context in which I see film is maybe a little different. I've worked a lot with image and movement: ballet, opera, theatre. These areas have in common a synthesis of the elements of movement, text, image and music. So when Godfrey Reggio asked me to work with him it was, from my point of view, simply another form to work in.

Film is peculiar however. There are several different kinds. We have, let's call them, "industry" films. When you're working in the "industry" then you're really working for the studio. There are some directors whose artistic wishes can prevail because of their stature and experience, like Scorsese. But they're rare.

1

4

5

6

(1–10) **Mishima**: Glass read every book of Yukio Mishima's before embarking on the project, including 'Sun and Steel', which talks about Mishima's suicide before it took place.

7

2

3

8

9

10

Mishima: The film was a "life in four chapters"; the black-and-white parts represent Yukio Mishima's life, and the colour parts (the fantasies) are from his novels. Glass chose a string quartet for the biographical parts and fully scored music for the fantasy scenes: "The music would create a structure for the film."

(1–3) Glass began his work on **Kundun** before the filming began, spotting the film with Martin Scorsese: "The matching of music and image is something I'm intrigued by – my way of working is quite different to that of other composers, I suppose."

Independent films are a bit different. If a studio doesn't like a film score they'll throw it out and hire another composer. Independent film-makers don't do that, they don't have limitless amounts of money. So, therefore, the work becomes much more collaborative.

Then, of course, you have the experimental film-makers like Godfrey Reggio and all kinds of in-between people like Paul Schrader. The convention of film-making, obviously, is that the artistic decisions are primarily made by the director. But Godfrey Reggio and I entered the project as equals. With Godfrey, the process was that he had images and I had music. Sometimes the music came first, sometimes Godfrey had a dramaturgical outline of what he wanted to do. He would produce masses of imagery which would then be put into assemblages of imagery, which would then be turned into rough cuts, so that it fitted an overall plan. This method allowed us to work side by side on **Koyaanisqatsi**, although Godfrey was mostly in California in order to access the film world technology.

Powaqqatsi I think we might have done in New York. We had a screening room set up at the end of every work period, which could be as short as a day. I would write music and take it to my studio. I have a group of very wonderful musicians like Michael Riesman who is a conductor and performer and he would assemble a work tape. Based on that we would then show the picture. At that point the editors would begin cutting the film to the work tape but we would also put the work tape to the film. It could go either way. I

even in some cases experimented with anticipating the cinematography by writing the music before it was filmed. I was interested in the process. **Powaqqatsi** begins with a scene from the Serra Pelada mines in Brazil. I looked at other footage of that setting. Originally I wrote ten minutes to set the scene and then we made a work tape and flew down with the whole crew, listening to the tape while filming at the mines. These films have a documentary style in that they are shot in the real world. People at the mines wanted to hear the music and were interested in what we were doing. So, on that occasion I was actually able to reverse what is considered the normal way of working. I also did that with **Kundun**.

Martin Scorsese and I talked about **Kundun** a month before he went to shoot it in Morocco and I began writing music to the scenario. We spotted the film on the basis of the scenario, not on the basis of a finished film. I sent the music to him in Morocco and he played it for the actors and listened to it on the set. The interesting thing about this method is that it should be seen as unusual. What I'm doing isn't strange, it is in fact the only way to make music and images work together organically and for this to happen they must come into the world at the same time. As to which comes first, it becomes like, "after you monsieur"…it doesn't matter. When the collaboration is happening on that level anyone can go first.

I presented this model of working to Marty and he was intrigued by it, but he had never done it. He said, "Well, how will we do it?" I said, "Let me score it, I'll send you the music and then we'll see what happens". Then he got very involved

philip glass

1

film music

3

2

4

5

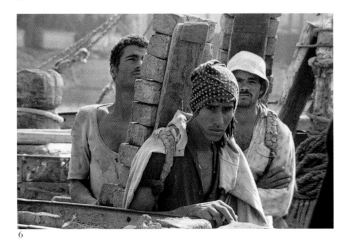

6

(1–6) **Powaqqatsi**: (2) Glass' strategy in **Powaqqatsi** was to create music that was very far from the image, an unbridgeable gap between audience and the picture. This was to emphasise the contrast between traditional societies and the transformations they have had to endure: "The music I wrote for the scenes with men working in the Serra Pelada mines is not slow and lethargic but quick and light." (7–8) **Koyaanisqatsi**: The film, whose title means "life out of balance" criticises our commodity-driven society through an apocalyptic vision.

7

8

with it until we got to the point of the film where the music was not ready because I was touring – in this case the "escape" scene, the last 20 minutes. He was willing to say, "Come back and do the music so I can go forward".

The way Marty works is he'll edit the whole picture and then he'll edit the same scene ten times. So then we have to go back and re-edit the music. Some of the scenes were done over and over again. The scene where the little boy is choosing his clothing was constantly changed. I had created this motif where you hear the cymbals and the drums. There's a kind of suspense music while he's thinking and then the cymbals and the drums come in. So every time he changed it I had to move them to a different place. Although we worked on **Kundun** for 14 months, Marty is such a master, and his command of visual language is so complete, that despite those frustrations working with him was most exciting.

The more general aspect of image and music is understanding what the parameters of that relationship are. As an analogy you can think of a physical description, of music being close to an image or far away from an image. Or you can think of music as being right on top of an image or being behind it or above it or below it. In fact the relationship of the image to the music is a precise one. For example, the music for **Powaqqatsi**'s Serra Pelada, where the image is of men working in the mines, is not slow and lethargic, heavy music. It's actually very quick, light music, and very rhythmic. Sometimes you want to work away from the image. The worst thing is the "Mickey Mousing" where for every image there's a

musical move. That happens when you look at a cartoon and Daffy Duck hits somebody over the head and you hear "clunk!" It doesn't provide any space for the spectator to enter the experience of watching. Commercials, jingles, are almost always done where the image and the music are right on top of each other... and it's done for propaganda purposes. The intention of the jingle director is to control your seeing so the music doesn't leave any space for you.

The other way, by contrast, is when you leave a certain space between the image and the music and the spectator has to psychologically cover that space. It's in the act of traversing that space that their experience becomes personalised. This is a cognitive process that we all undertake and the skill lies in measuring that distance.

Where, in **Powaqqatsi**, there are scenes of television commercials and snippets of television, Godfrey was presenting the worst nightmare of modern media technology. We've gone from the villages of Peru and India to the advanced world of high communications where what you're looking at is complete garbage. And so the music is an alienated music. It is a music that does not invite you to the image because you don't want to be part of it. I use the word "alienated" because I think the malaise of contemporary life is that feeling of being cut off from the world. The danger in working with Godfrey's kind of messages is that they are so direct and articulate that to underscore the message is to kill the message. The music and images could not be saying the same thing entirely because if they did they would be

The Truman Show: Glass actually appears in this film playing the violin on a piece he composed for the film, 'Truman Sleeps'.

1

2

3

4

(1–4) **Dracula**: Glass was asked by Universal pictures to write a score for the 1931 version of **Dracula** starring Bela Lugosi: "Theatre and opera are interpretative art forms, film is not. I wanted to allow for re-interpretation in film. I'm proposing film as a performance work where we're not talking about music as background – it's music with film and not film with music. The partnership between music and image becomes unmistakable. The whole function of watching is different, the whole emotional effect of a piece is quite different also. We can say things in music that are never said in the works."

unwatchable. So, I tried to do a complicated dance around the images, of being close to them and far away and the music is constantly shifting this point of view.

Mishima was really my first narrative movie and I wanted to carry over the techniques which I had been honing with Godfrey. I needed a method which I used a lot in the theatre where I work with the writer and the designer and surround myself with as much sensory data as I can, whether it's word or image. I asked Eiko Ishioka for all her drawings and I pinned them on the wall of my studio while I was composing.

Paul Schrader gave me a lot of room about where I could put the music. He calls the film, "a life in four chapters". The black-and-white parts are the biographical past of Yukio Mishima and the colour parts are from the novels. The device of the film is that the film and his life gradually come together so that his life and art become one thing. I suggested to Paul that the music should be as follows: the black-and-white part should be string quartet and that this would represent his biography; the more fully scored music would represent the scenes from the novels and that at the end we would take the themes that had been biographical and give them a full orchestration. The music became a container that Paul and I could work in. He invited me to become a kind of co-author in the sense that the music would function structurally.

What interests me about theatre and opera is the fact that these are interpretative art forms and what's curious about film is that it's not. When you make a film, it's done. So there's

something very poignant about that. I began to think of how a film could be interpreted. I took on a project which allows for the possibility of re-interpretation. I managed to get the rights to turn the volume down on the original soundtrack of three Cocteau films (**La Belle et la Bête; Les Enfants terribles; Orphée**) and to play my music. What I'm doing, therefore, can only be done live.

I've invented a number of ways of working around the frustrations and conventions of the industry, where film can be part of performance, where it can be dynamic, where it can work and where the impact on the audience is immeasurably higher than you would find otherwise.

biography

Born in Toronto, Canada, in 1946 Howard Shore studied at the Berklee School of Music in Boston. He began life as a professional musician touring with the rock group Lighthouse in the late '60s, after which he became the first music director of TV's *Saturday Night Live* before embarking on a career of full-time film composing. He initially worked on low-budget pieces, significantly with the director David Cronenberg (**The**

howard shore

Brood, 1979; **Scanners**, 1980; **Videodrome**, 1982; **The Fly**, 1986; **Dead Ringers**, 1988; **Naked Lunch**, 1991; **M. Butterfly**, 1993; **Crash**, 1996; **eXistenZ**, 1999). After his beginnings with Cronenberg, he moved towards scoring for major productions such as **After Hours** (1986, Martin Scorsese); **The Silence of the Lambs** (1990) and **Philadelphia** (1993), both directed by Jonathan Demme; **Ed Wood** (1994, Tim Burton); and **Seven** (1995) and **The Game** (1997), both directed by David Fincher. Other films include **Big** (1986, Penny Marshall); **Mrs Doubtfire** (1995, Chris Columbus); **Looking for Richard** (1996, Al Pacino) and **Analyze This** (1999, Harold Ramis). His most recent work is **Dogma** (1999, Kevin Smith).

interview

I studied at the Berklee School of Music in Boston. It gave me the foundation for writing, orchestration and composition. Then I was on the road playing rock and roll for four years with the group Lighthouse until I was 22. It was the late '60s' music revolution and we toured with the Grateful Dead and Jefferson Airplane. We opened for Jimi Hendrix at the Isle of Wight Festival. I played the sax. The sound was modelled after groups like Blood Sweat and Tears, i.e. a rock rhythm section and a horn section. But we had something different – a string section, an electric string quartet. The viola player, Don Dinovo, was 20 years older than me and he had a great knowledge of 20th-century music. He made me aware of Schoenberg, Berg and Webern. When I got off the road I met and collaborated with some theatre people in Toronto and began working for the Canadian Broadcasting Corporation. The group I was working with moved down to New York in 1975 and created the *Saturday Night Live* show. I did that for five years and then got into film music.

1

2

3

4

5

6

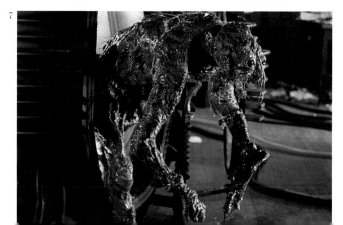

7

(1–3) **Dead Ringers**: "Everything had to move in a very specific way. I wanted to match the cinematography, production design, lighting and acting. The colours were very specific – the grey's precise. I wanted the score to have a black-and-white quality." (4–7) **The Fly**. (4) Orchestral short score of the cue 'Run Up Stairs'. An "action" line describing what's happening in the film runs across the top of each stave. The music is scored just for strings which mingle in a dissonant fashion, but which then settle down to almost no movement at around bar nine.

I'd worked on a Canadian feature in 1978 but it was working with David Cronenberg that I got the opportunity to try things I was really interested in. I thought film music might be a good way to express myself creatively. Like theatre, it was collaborative. It had a director, actors, a writer and a musician. It was the context I was used to. It seemed like a natural way to work and experiment at the same time. Being involved with David on those early films like **The Brood, Scanners, Videodrome**, was real guerilla film-making. You could do whatever you wanted. There wasn't much money around so everyone was happy. Those scores were often written after one viewing of the film. I would live and breathe the feeling of it for about a week and I'd write a lot of music, trying to get into some subconscious level of composing. This is a very dreamy period when I'm just thinking of the imagery of the film and how it affects me and how I might match it musically. I'll record a lot of music at that point, mostly improvisation. Then I'll spend another week analysing it, trying to understand what I was feeling and what I created and what I could use in the film.

It was a different musical starting point for **The Silence of the Lambs**. I began by reading the script. Then I looked at a few cuts of the film and met with Jonathan Demme a few times prior to the actual spotting session. The spotting was very important on that film as contextually the music had to focus on the Jodie Foster character, Clarice Starling. It has a lot of emotional depth and a real subtext which Jonathan directed me towards. In the opening section where she goes for a run the music, in a sense, describes her relationship with Lecter. It's very dramatic and you're made to concentrate on her emotional side. You follow her through the story with the music. Eventually Starling knocks on Gumb's door at the end – that suburban house by the railway track – and he opens the door and she's in the living room; a moth flies in the room and suddenly she discovers it's him, the man she's been searching for the entire film. At that moment of realisation the music becomes very operatic and it's actually quite beautiful but with a lot of darkness in it. I love that scene. There are electronic ambiences mixed in to create a kind of ghost score.

Once I've written a score I'll programme the computer, take the notes of the score and programme very non-tonal sounds. I've been doing this for many years. I think in **The Silence of the Lambs** there's quite a lot of underwater whale sounds that have been slowed down. The computer plays these sounds, along with the orchestra, based on the notes in the score in a very condensed version. So if the orchestration suddenly grows larger in one spot the computer will also do that, but it may do it a few bars later because the notes are triggering sounds that might have a long pre-delay before you even hear them. It's quite a random process that follows the general shape of the orchestration, yet it creates an unease and you're not really quite sure why.

With **Naked Lunch** there was some manipulation of the sound in the editing, some overlapping things that I created which connects with the cut and paste technique that Burroughs used in the book. Some of Ornette Coleman's music is superimposed over certain pieces that I wrote and

1

3

(1–8) **Naked Lunch**: "The chronology of this film isn't linear – it's out of sequence." (5–6) Two versions of the same 'Main Title' cue. On the right Shore's sketch with orchestration notes. In his notes at the bottom of the page he clarifies his thoughts to orchestrator Homer Denison. On the left Denison's final orchestration. "The orchestra is playing a slow kind of tango, very exotic with a lush, somewhat erotic atmosphere, but over this you have Ornette Coleman playing sax very quickly to a much faster rhythm than the orchestra."

4

2

©1991 · Howard Shore, SFA (ASCAP)

5   6   7

8

1

2

film music

(1–7) **The Silence of the Lambs**: "Sometimes women musicians come up to me when I do orchestral recordings. It's amazing how many of them felt **The Silence of the Lambs** to be an emotional experience. I think they felt something partly because of the way the music focused on Starling, the Jodie Foster character."

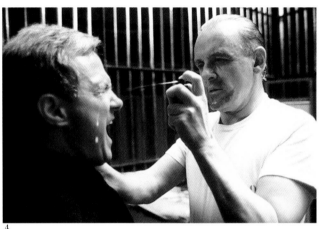

4

3

The Silence of the Lambs: (7) Shore's sketch with orchestration notes for the cue 'The Beating'. The piano part above the strings is Shore's composition with a timpani part and notes for the brass added. From this Homer Denison has filled out the final orchestration. And these orchestrations are often densely packed with instruments performing at the lower limits of their register. This often helps to evoke an unsettling feeling and at other times sheer terror.

vice-versa but I would say that about 90 per cent of what you hear is live. I tried a lot of different things and after about a month of editing and mixing I went back to the live recordings with the orchestra and Ornette.

I approached the score by reading the book and thinking about the period and geography – New York and Morocco, be-bop jazz and North African music. I remembered a recording Ornette Coleman had made in the '60s with Berber musicians. I played it to Cronenberg and he loved it and thought it could be the Interzone National Anthem. I also started working with tapes that Dean Benedetti had made of Charlie Parker performances. I looped them and made little pieces out of them. I played Ornette the Parker stuff and asked him if he wanted to re-record it but he felt it was definitive and suggested he should write some other trio pieces for the movie as well as playing on my score with the London Philharmonic. So, I based the score on the Parker loops and then worked with Ornette for a week until finally he came in and improvised with the orchestra.

I wanted the opening title music to take people right into the world of the movie. The orchestra is playing a very slow kind of tango, very exotic with a lush, somewhat erotic atmosphere, but over this you have Ornette playing very quickly to a much faster rhythm than the orchestra. So you have the dreamy orchestra taking you down the rabbit hole and Ornette blasting your brain with little bits of be-bop and the craziness of it all. Some of the scenes in the movie were created with overlapping techniques and the music mirrors this. For the

scene in the apartment with Joan where he calls her a junkie and says she's no good and then tells her he loves her, I recorded Monk's 'Misterioso' which Ornette arranged. Then I also wrote a piece to accompany that, except it's not really accompanying, it's on another level. There's a lot going on in the score though it's not really to do with individual characters but with creating a feeling for the movie.

In **Ed Wood** I tried to give the orchestration a kind of "Ed-Woodness". The idea that nothing could be wrong. In the Ed Wood world, good and bad were the same in a way, there was an optimism and a kind of make-do sense. Tim Burton creates his own world and invites you in to play and that period of '50s jazz, Cuban music, was just perfect for me to work in. Tim and I did some fairly extensive spotting sessions on the film as to where the music should be used. I was overflowing with ideas so the process of elimination became important. Once I'd decided on certain elements like the use of the theremin and a lot of percussion then I could create the particular sound of the film.

The orchestration is from a million different styles of period stuff: horror movies, stripper music, bongo music, Henry Mancini. I used a 45-piece group, like the Universal horror music orchestra and a Novachord organ, like they had in the '50s. But, of course, it was all going through my imagination, my concept, my melodies and harmonies.

I think the opening animation is choreographed brilliantly. The animators created a mock-up with Tim and then I wrote

1

2

4

(1–4) **Ed Wood**: "Tim sent me some of Ed Wood's movies and I screened them. Once I had the imagery I thought of all the sounds of the '50s: jazz, Cuban music, horror music. I used a lot of percussion. There's a seven-piece percussion section playing the main title. There's a lot of optimism in the score, like Ed Wood himself."

howard shore

3

1

film music

2

5

6

(1–7) **Ed Wood**: (2–6) The first five pages of Howard Shore's conductor's score for the 'Main Title' of **Ed Wood**: "The opening title is a very rhythmic, very choreographed piece. The animation is brilliant and it takes you into the world of the film very quickly." Note the exotic instrumentation: marimba, vibraphone, bongo and conga, pipe organ, and on page two, bar six, the entry of the theremin main theme. Note also at the top of the score that Howard Shore orchestrated this highly colourful score himself. "I used a 45-piece group, like the Universal horror music orchestra and a Novachord organ, like they had in the '50s. But of course it was all going through my imagination, my concept, my melodies and harmonies." (7) Howard Shore's worksheet of themes for **Ed Wood**.

1

2

(1–2) **eXistenZ**: In his score for this film Shore was expressing the idea of aural perception: "This film is about virtual reality and I was attempting a virtual aural experience. The orchestra was recorded in a way that played with the listener's perception of what an orchestra should sound like." (right top) Howard Shore conducting. (right bottom) A recording session.

the piece. I think it was tweaked a little afterwards to keep that rhythmic flow. It's imagery and music working really well together, taking you into the world of the film. Another scene where image and music blend really well is in the funeral scene where Bela Lugosi dies and you hear Tchaikovsky's 'Dying Swan' theme from 'Swan Lake', which is also a quote from **Dracula** (1931, Tod Browning). I added my own melodies and some of the odd '50s instruments like the theremin. I think the symbolism worked really well.

Even though I compose with pen and paper and I have to see the relationship of the notes in black and white, I can sort of feel the music and hear the weight of it. It's not so much an intellectual process. Sidney Lumet paid me the greatest compliment in his book, 'Making Movies'. He said he liked the score to **The Silence of the Lambs** because he could feel it. I know what he meant. It's not so much about hearing the music in the cinema when you're watching the scene; it's that you can feel it.

biography

Born in L.A. in 1954 Elfman began composing for film in 1985 while a founder member of the rock group Oingo Boingo. He began an informal partnership with Tim Burton started with **Pee-Wee's Big Adventure**. He is recognised for a witty, surreal and highly post-modern style of scoring which often refers to the classic Hollywood period of Herrmann whilst at the same time embracing contemporary

danny elfman

ideas. Danny Elfman has composed scores for almost all of Tim Burton's films to date (**Pee-Wee's Big Adventure**, 1985; **Beetlejuice**, 1988; **Batman**, 1989; **Edward Scissorhands**, 1990; **Batman Returns**, 1992; **The Nightmare before Christmas**, 1993; **Mars Attacks!**, 1996; **Sleepy Hollow**, 1999). Other major Hollywood productions he has written scores for include **Dick Tracy** (1990, Warren Beatty); **Sommersby** (1993, Jon Amiel); **To Die For** (1995, Gus Van Sant); **Mission: Impossible** (1996, Brian de Palma); and **Men in Black** (1997, Barry Sonnenfeld). An instant example of the Elfman style can be heard almost daily on a global basis in his brilliant and virtuosic theme for the TV cartoon series *The Simpsons*.

interview

I grew up in L.A. in the '60s, around the block from the movie theatre where I spent all my free time. It's there that I really discovered film. Cinema for my gang consisted primarily of horror, science fiction and fantasy, preferably the bloodier the better, and absolutely nothing with singing and dancing or, God forbid, romance – not uncommon for boys in that period. It was during a screening of **The Day the Earth Stood Still** (1951, Robert Wise) that I first became aware of film music and of an artist who created the film music – Bernard Herrmann. At that moment I realised that the music moved me, and that it was a human, personal artistic effort, not some music machine that turned it out. From that point on, if I saw Bernard Herrmann's name in the beginning of a movie, I knew there was something special, something extra, and I think that's where my love of film music began.

It was a bit ironic that as a teenager I thought I would end up as a cinematographer, an editor, perhaps even a director. I

1

3

4

(1–4) **Beetlejuice**: Elfman felt that he had cemented his feelings about theme versus style by the time he came to work on **Beetlejuice**. (2) The waiting room scene gave Elfman the chance to invoke a lounge-like feel: "Tim [Burton] and I had a fondness for a strong Dean Martin influence which I really enjoyed doing. Sometimes I do little gag versions of a piece of music and lounge-ise it, and Tim really loves that."

film music

2

loved film but I always felt more aligned with the visual side. Although I appreciated the music very much it never occurred to me that that would be my calling. My elementary school music teacher declared almost immediately when I attempted to play trombone that I had no musical propensity whatsoever, and I think I believed her for quite a long time. Later as a teenager I took lessons on a few instruments, but never with much luck, as I seemed to really lack the discipline to sit in front of a single teacher and play for them – in fact I became almost phobic about it. However, what I did learn during those lessons was that I had a good memory for music. I would often memorise the early melody books and play them back without actually reading them. My first performance was on the violin at the age of 18 in France with a musical troupe called the Grand Magic Circus. It was quite accidental that I ended up with them. My brother was already a member, and I had only been playing the violin for four months at that point, but the director thought I was good and I went on the road with them. And it was also for them that I played my first composition, which was done for mandolin. After spending a year in West Africa, which cemented my love of percussion and ethnic music which I still care for to this day, I joined my brother in L.A. with a theatrical troupe called the Mystic Nights of the Oingo Boingo. That was where my musical training really began. During seven or eight years with them I was forced to teach myself to write. Also, we did a lot of arrangements of 1930s' jazz like Duke Ellington, Cab Calloway, Django Rheinhart – I became a bit obsessed with transcribing solos absolutely correctly and I think that's where I got my best ear training. I remember distinctly listening to an old recording of Duke Ellington's 'Black and Tan Fantasy' and transcribing all the parts, especially the piano solo which was actually quite difficult and being able to get it absolutely correct. It did a lot for my confidence because I learned I could hear a phrase and write it down just right.

In 1985 I met Tim Burton and Pee-Wee Herman, aka Paul Rubens, when they asked me if I was interested in writing the score for **Pee-Wee's Big Adventure**. I was baffled why they wanted me. Although I had done a wild cult film for my brother five years earlier, I never expected it to lead to a legitimate orchestral film score. But even though I thought they were crazy talking to me because I lacked the training I did have a vibe about the movie. I didn't connect at all with the comedic musical styles of that time and my feeling was that Pee Wee was not an American contemporary character. Maybe it was the bike race at the beginning that led me to Nino Rota as my influence, I don't know, but it felt right. I wrote a piece of music for them never expecting anything to come from it and that piece of music ended up becoming the main title for the film.

It was doing **Pee-Wee's Big Adventure** that really got me hooked on film scoring. Being a comedy it had lots of very specific action and it was not uncommon in a two-minute cue to be hitting 30 or 40 hits. In the beginning that was very difficult, but what I really learned was that I could not only do it, but do it really well. I was able to find the rhythm of the editor, and write in such a way that made it look like he was cutting to my music, which is how music of that genre should

1

(1–5) **Batman**: This was Danny Elfman's first big feature film: he would go on to score the sequel, **Batman Returns**, also directed by Tim Burton. (1–2) Burton associated 'Beautiful Dreamer' with the Joker: "I was in complete agreement and really enjoyed blending it in. It's a pleasure to have some light moments to fall into when there is so much music." (3) In spite of having to write a love theme for the romance between Vicky Vail and Batman, Elfman felt the real romance was more to do with "Batman's own dark impulses". (4–5) Elfman based the car chase on 'Carmina Burana'. It also gave him the opportunity to write choral music: "I love writing for choir – it's just another instrument for me."

2

3

4

danny elfman

5

(4–6) **Edward Scissorhands**: The opening cue of Danny Elfman's orchestral score: "I'd been writing a lot of busy music for busy movies and it was such a pleasure to do this film where there's this simple storyline and simple characters." (6) The entry of the wordless choir as the strings play pizzicato, creating a very ethereal, open orchestral texture.

(1–3) **Batman**: The opening page of the full orchestral score of the cue 'Cathedral Chase'. Note the credit for Elfman's regular orchestrator Steve Bartek: "Steve understands my music very well, and knows not to elaborate on it in a way that I am not going to want." Note also the pipe organ part denoting location. The rough annotation of on-screen action (rear shot... steps...) above the violin part is for the conductor to synchronise to film as the orchestra plays. Elfman's rich, colourful music harks back to the grandeur of Korngold's scores, and perfectly complements Tim Burton's vision of Gotham City.

3

(1–6) **Edward Scissorhands**: (1) The influence for the haircutting scene was a gypsy piece: "It started Spanish gypsy, then became Hungarian and then went back to Spanish again." (4) For the suburban scenes Elfman wanted to invoke a lounge feel "like Escovel". In many ways, the score has an almost religious sensitivity: "I wasn't trying to be religious but I think that the ethereal side of a fairy tale can cross into quasi-religious tones. I think that probably goes back to my ballet music influences."

feel if done correctly. I remember the first day at the scoring stage hearing the first cue – it was the bicycle race. It was only a medium-sized orchestra, but yet, it was one of the biggest, most exciting sounds I had ever heard. It was like an injection or something – and it really got to me.

I suppose it was very lucky that I started out with Tim, and we developed an affinity right away. I don't really know why that is. I seem to really understand his film-making, where he is coming from, and most importantly, the unusual and difficult musical tones that his movies seem to have. Also, it makes me very pleased when a film comes along that is visual and theatrical, and I get to express myself in a grander, more operatic, ballet or theatrical style. I like writing with broad strokes on a big canvas when I can.

I saw there was this chance to write a very ambitious score for **Batman**. It was Tim's and my first big action feature and the producers were, I think, a bit sceptical about my ability, and rightly so. I really had to prove myself. I had to mock-up all the cues and play them for everybody – I sweated blood to prove my abilities on that film. I will never forget the day when the producer hearing the first cue began jumping up and down, waving his arms like he was conducting with his baton. At that moment I knew that I had succeeded in winning them over.

Batman may have been the first time I used a choir as strongly as I did. I remember there was a moment when you first see the Batmobile and it drives to the batcave and that

was the first big choir piece, very reminiscent of 'Carmina Burana', and I will never forget the excitement of hearing the choir sing that piece. I have been using choir ever since then – I suppose it has become one of my signature devices. I happen to love choral music; my favourite parts of most operas are the choral pieces between the major arias, and that's what I will play over and over for myself. The choral music of Mozart, his requiem, of Carl Orff and of Fauré were very big influences on me, as was the exciting, propulsive music of Stravinsky, Prokofiev, and Tchaikovsky. I seem to have a strong Russian and Eastern European bent that I can never totally remove myself from. After **Batman** a lot of people asked me about my Wagnerian influences and my answer was that I never really listened to Wagner. On the other hand I was very influenced by other composers such as Korngold, Tiomkin and Steiner and I think they were probably very much influenced by Wagner, so I probably was indirectly. Many of my musical influences are classical which have in fact been filtered through other film composers.

It's also in that period between **Beetlejuice**, **Batman** and **Edward Scissorhands** that I really began to cement my own feelings of theme versus style. If there's no theme it's just lots of orchestration, and it could be a brilliant orchestration but it's really only a huge temp score to me. On the other hand if it is nothing but theme it becomes monotonous and that doesn't work either. If you look at the composers of the Golden Age they understood it perfectly – the balance between theme, style and orchestration – planting the seeds of the theme so you could use it full-grown when you want at the

2

(1–2) **The Nightmare before Christmas**: Even though the film only lasts 75 minutes, the scoring was a two-and-a-half-year project, as the film contained no less than ten separate themes. Paul Rubens, Catherine O'Hara and Danny Elfman's voices featured on the tracks: "One night I cut every song and did the voices – all the synth tracks with instrumentals – so now we had demos to synth music with clicks, and that's what they used to animate."

(1–3) **Mars Attacks!**: Elfman saw the rough cut and initial main titles for the film quite early on and was immediately inspired as to what would be the main title. He structured it around two themes: the Prokofiev-style March signalled the oncoming ships of the aliens and a theremin was used to denote an extra science-fiction element. He likens the music to the style of that in **The Day the Earth Stood Still**, a film scored by Bernard Herrmann.

end of the film. Ultimately I think a composer's real style and certainly my own isn't the writing of the theme but what you do with it – how you take it, turn it inside out.

With **Edward Scissorhands** everything happened very organically and simply, quite the opposite of **Batman**. What I loved about writing that score, and it's one of my favourites, was that it was a very simple through-line. I'd been in a period of writing some very busy music for films, and often forcing things in to try to enhance something that might not be there, a very common job for a composer, so it was a pleasure to do **Edward Scissorhands** where this simple storyline was told from an internal standpoint of this one charcter, and musically I simply had to follow that. I think the film was clearly an old-fashioned, sweet fairy tale and I think I played it just as I saw it. Also the music was very sappy and romantic and emotional and I enjoy doing that. I love it when it's really intense, really violent, really sappy, actually just about really anything. When it's none of those things I struggle and die and flop about in the water and feel like I'm drowning.

Playing the music for the first time for the director is still one of the most terrifying experiences that I could possibly imagine – even Tim, who I believe I have done nine films with already. In **Edward Scissorhands**, for example, there are two primary themes, not one, which is very unusual. One of them had a very Eastern European, Hungarian bent, and I had no idea how Tim was going to react. Many directors, in fact, would say "this music is making me feel this character is Eastern European, so it's wrong" but people are very forgiving

that way and Tim fortunately doesn't think that way either. He thinks much more on a visceral level and the music worked for him viscerally, so it didn't matter to him what its origins were. Tim is very clear but not verbal in most of our communications. I actually prefer that – when a director starts trying to explain in musical terms what he or she is looking for it usually leads to confusion, but Tim and I generally speak in emotional terms. He tells me how he feels about the characters and scenes and how he feels about the music.

I think my greatest joy in writing a film score is the many surprises that happen during the process. I never try to intellectualise my music and when a particular variation on a theme wants to happen at a particular point, I let it. Before I begin writing I have to do a lot of homework. I take the themes that I'm thinking of using and put then through a kind of acid test to see if they can turn emotional, whimsical, dramatic or funny. I'll try blocking out two or three major themes until I feel really confident that the themes are going to work for me. After that, of course, they evolve themselves and go wherever they want to go. In **Sleepy Hollow** I was shocked that a theme I had written for Johnny Depp's child character – it was originally a children's theme – kept popping up for the headless horseman, often at its most maniacal moments, yet it worked. I think it goes back to the feeling that there really are no rules. That's what I learned from listening to Bernard Herrmann's scores between the science-fiction films that he did and the romantic films and the Hitchcock films. Anything can work if it is done well.

biography

Born in 1955 Zbigniew Preisner is Poland's leading film composer. Between the years 1985 and 1996 he enjoyed a close collaboration with the director Krzysztof Kieslowski and his script writer Krzysztof Piesiewicz. His scores for Kieslowski's films have brought him international acclaim as well as numerous awards. These include two Cesars from the French Film Academy and three consecutive citations as the year's most outstanding film composer in The L.A.

zbigniew preisner

Critics Association Awards of 1991, 1992 and 1993. In 1992 he received the Award of the Minister of Foreign Affairs for outstanding achievements in the presentation of Polish Culture abroad. Around the world his soundtrack albums for Kieslowski's films have sold over one million copies. His film scores include the short film series **Dekalog 1–10**, (1988); **The Double Life of Véronique** (1991); **Three Colours: Blue** (1993); **Three Colours: White** (1993); and **Three Colours: Red** (1994); all directed by Krzysztof Kieslowski. Other important scores are **Europa, Europa** (1991, Agnieszka Holland); **At Play in the Fields of the Lord** (1991, Hector Babenco); **Damage** (1992, Louis Malle); **The Secret Garden** (1993, Agnieszka Holland); **When A Man Loves A Woman** (1994, Luis Mandoki); **Fairytale – A True Story** (1997, Charles Sturridge); and more recently **The Last September** (1999, Deborah Warner) and **Aberdeen** (2000, Hans Petter Moland).

interview

My father was an amateur musician who played the accordion at weddings and birthday parties; music was part of everyday life so I didn't study it, instead I studied history and art at the university in Krakow. Then I joined a political cabaret, where people wrote topical songs about the world they lived in. I played the piano, wrote and sang songs and then I taught myself music theory and compositional techniques from text books; I was very much influenced by the leader of this group. The people who surround you are more important than what you are inspired by. I'm not inspired by music, I'm interested in literature, philosophy, life, painting, people. I happened to grow up with folk music from which there is so much to be learned, but when you're composing music you're never sure where it comes from.

I try and write emotionally and not mechanically; it's always important to understand how the narrative in a film relates to music. But for me the most important thing in music is

1

3

4

(1–4) **The Double Life of Véronique**: Preisner's score for this film is a good example of his instrumental economy; he uses what is required and nothing more. The main theme is played almost solely by woodwinds and many of the others are written for piano and guitar.

film music

2

silence. And in order for the silence to play, one has to prepare it with something before and after. You'll hear a lot of silence in my scores.

My approach now, once I've received the brief from the director, is to spot the music cues, develop ideas at the piano, and then write straight to paper; I rarely use any kind of synthesizers or sampling. But there is no straightforward recipe for writing film music. Sometimes I first compose the themes or sometimes I just think about textures which then become the basis of themes. The orchestration for me is inseparable from the film themes. Sometimes I narrow it down to a few instruments and at other times I go for a big orchestral sound.

I wrote music for many television films before I met Kieslowski. It was through scoring my first movie, **The Weather Forecast** (1981), that director Antoni Krauze recommended me to Krzysztof Kieslowski. Kieslowski and I developed an unusual way of working. We became friends and the music in his films was considered as part of the initial concept. At that time I was a young composer. When I was writing the music for 12 films in total (**Dekalog** and two feature films), it was my ambition to write completely different music for each film. I wanted to prove my ability to write music in various styles. Something I've always liked is the feeling of intimacy you get with music written for a few instruments. Obviously another very important issue at the time was how music and sound design could work together. All the time Kieslowski and I discussed how to achieve the perfect symbiosis of music and heightened natural sound effects. **Dekalog** was not filmed in the proper sequence from one to ten. The first one was **Dekalog 5 (A Short Film About Killing)** followed by **Dekalog 6 (A Short Film About Love)**. Music recording for those two films was separate. The recording for the remaining **Dekalog** films was divided into just three recording sessions.

In **Dekalog 9 (Thou shalt not Covet thy Neighbour's Wife)** the main character, Dorota, has a moment of revelation in her flat and she puts a record on. We thought about using a classical recording of some kind but we decided that it was better that I would write a piece of music. And having done it we decided to invent a composer as if this composer existed – that was how Van den Budenmayer came into being; it was a red herring. But then the idea developed – that Van den Budenmayer could crop up in each of the films. In fact there are references to him in **The Double Life of Véronique** (he is credited with the 'Concerto in E minor') right through to **Three Colours: Blue** where Julie (Juliette Binoche) listens to some of his vocal music in a record shop booth. He became an alter-ego.

I think the success of my music started with my scores for Kieslowski's films. The music was on a borderline. It wasn't classical music but at the same time it wasn't film music. I make creative music; the times of dodecaphonic music of the 20th century, of difficult music, have ended. What has replaced it now is some kind of romanticism. I like to work with the same orchestra – Sinfonia Varsovia. I noticed that the

1

2

film music

3

5

6

(1) Zbigniew Preisner at his mixing desk. (2–6) **Damage**: Preisner's score follows Jeremy Irons' British politician in his ruinous affair with his son's girlfriend, played by Juliette Binoche. Instead of a scene of sexual tension, Preisner opted for a classical sound to reflect the stuffiness of the English family. This counterpoints the action and makes the affair seem that much more "seedy".

1

3

2

4

5

(1–5) **A Short Film about Love**: "Another very important issue at the time (of **Dekalog**) was how music and sound design could work together. For me, the music and film effects are one." This desire for cohesion may account for Preisner having recorded eight of the ten **Dekalog** film scores in only three sessions.

8

6

9

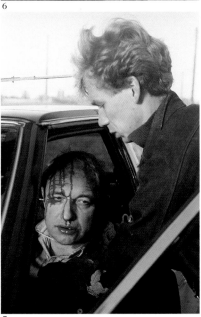
7

(6–9) **A Short Film about Killing**: Preisner wrote the scores for **Dekalog** as a young composer, and wanted to prove his ability to write music in various different styles. He and Kieslowski discussed at length to create perfect combinations of instrumental music and sound effects.

more we recorded together the faster the recordings became and I did not have to explain how to play their parts or how to phrase my melodies. They felt it automatically. They're very good, particularly the strings, at playing at the edge of the note. Often I write long single notes, which appear ambiguous, they're not quarter tones but they're hard to place; you hear them quite a lot in **Dekalog**. I'm also keen to work with Sinfonia Varsovia because I like recording in Poland, my homeland. You have to remember that in Poland nobody had passports until 1990. To get out of the country to work with any foreign organisation was a bureaucratic nightmare. Now, sometimes I like to record with orchestras in other countries, as these sessions often introduce fresh elements into the music. Generally, the choice of the orchestra depends on the kind of music I've composed.

Three Colours: Blue was the first of Kieslowski's trilogy exploring the themes of France's national motto: "Liberty, Equality and Fraternity". The music was 90 per cent composed and recorded before filming started. It was described in detail in Kieslowski's screenplay. Of course music is a central character in **Three Colours: Blue**. Patrice, an acclaimed European composer is killed in a car crash and his wife Julie spends much of the film escaping from and eventually coming to terms with his music. Krzysztof Kieslowski liked simple music, although played by a huge orchestra. That is why very often in order to stress the emotions and to achieve a strong effect I wrote in unison but in widely spaced octaves. It gives the impression that this music is very expansive and monumental. At one point Julie

and Patrice's assistant Olivier re-orchestrate Patrice's music and you hear the results instantly in the film score; you see, we were playing, showing how the character of the same music may be influenced by changing the instruments. Kieslowski thought that the best expression of the feelings or important experiences of his main characters should be through the music. This is metaphysical and nothing to do with acting. In other words, the music was to play the part of actors' internal emotions. It very often happens that when we experience the greatest joy or tragedy, we stay calm on the outside but we go through it really deeply inside. In Krzysztof's films the music was this inside. At scoring sessions Krzysztof very often reacted to my music by trying to bring out and highlight the most important thing for him — inner feelings.

In **Three Colours: White** the music score is completely ironic. When, finally, the hero arrives back in Warsaw and is thrown on to a garbage dump he surveys his surroundings and exclaims, "Home at last". The music becomes very like Chopin, a Polish cultural icon – it was ironic. At that time Poland was one huge garbage dump. The juxtaposition with the Chopin piano music was to emphasise this. That was also the idea behind the tango music which plays as the hero begins to gain strength. Tango in Poland is the dance for common people, ironic and primitive, yet at the same time it has a real forward momentum.

In the film **Three Colours: Red**, the main theme, 'Bolero', was written before filming. We wanted to stress the recurrence

1

2

3

4

5

6

(1) Zbigniew Preisner at his mixing desk in his studio. (2–6) **The Secret Garden**: Preisner recorded the music with the Sinfonia Varsovia and the boys' choir of the Cracovian Philharmonic: "The more we recorded together the faster the recordings were. They automatically felt the music." Preisner's music sometimes appears elementary and uncomplicated but this is often due to the ease with which the orchestra performs it.

1

2

4

3

(1–4) **Three Colours: White**: Some of Preisner's most structured and detailed music was written for this film. The music has a melancholic feel to it, with its sparse instrumentation: "All the music is ironic, reflecting the terrible state of Poland at that time."

5

6

8

(5–8) **Three Colours: Blue**: "90 per cent of the music was recorded before anything was filmed. It was described in detail in Krzysztof Kieslowski's screenplay." Preisner uses a big orchestral palette in short, broken cues, full of resonant colour. But despite the size of the instrumental forces it still retains a characteristic starkness, often due to widely spaced unison voicings.

zbigniew preisner

7

1

(1–4) **Three Colours: Red:** Preisner chose to write a rich, melodic score based on a 'Bolero' theme. The repetition in the 'Bolero' form, with its increased expression for each repetition, is used to represent the recurrence of life situations and events. (right) Zbigniew Preisner.

3

2

4

of situations and events in our lives. Bolero is a musical form based on the repetition of the theme, with increased expression after each repetition. It was supposed to be the music about the will to fight, the will to live, the unexpectedness of events and the willingness to discover more about other people. The **Three Colours** series was three different films and the music and its themes were not meant to be interrelated.

Nothing has happened accidentally in my life. Since Krzysztof Kieslowski's death in 1996 I've become more interested in writing music independently of film. That is why I have felt the need to meet new people, new musicians, because they inspire me. As a composer it's important to find musicians with strong personalities. It's like the casting process for a film director. My leading actors are the musicians of the orchestra – and without doubt they convey the character of the music. My first consideration is what to talk about and then, depending on the subject, how to say it. Sometimes it may be a kind of music monodrama or a small musical discussion, another time an orchestral storm. I have never used an orchestrator. It would inevitably create misunderstandings, since I have no idea how I could define the boundaries between my creation and somebody else's. Of course I like it very much when my musical themes are rearranged, but then it's no longer me driving this car. I am only a passenger.

Hollywood now tries to stifle any individuality in music. The main preoccupation there is writing music that will appeal to everybody. This is the difference between Europe and Hollywood. In Europe the director and his team usually take a risk in presenting their individual view. They are artistically free. But the director is the one ultimately responsible for the results. In Hollywood it is not totally clear who creates the film and who is responsible for it.

I have never thought about moving to America. I remember one occasion when, for the third time, I received an American Critics Award; it was for my score for **Damage**. Right after the ceremony I had a meeting with the president of Warner Brothers, the company for which I'd scored **The Secret Garden**. While congratulating me on the Award and stressing its importance in America, he tried to persuade me that, as I was in Hollywood, I should start composing in a more American style. For me it was like – to stay with the car analogy – driving the car forwards and backwards at the same time. An absurd situation. Progress in every field of life, which includes art, is founded on rebellion and setting up new trends, new directions. It's impossible to do that if you constantly look back to old reference points.

175

biography

Born in January 1952, Sakamoto studied composition at the Tokyo National University of Fine Arts and Music. In 1978 he became a founder member of the Yellow Magic Orchestra. One of the earliest techno-pop groups, they gained a huge international following. Sakamoto's first film score was for **Merry Christmas, Mr Lawrence**. Four years later he was awarded an Oscar for the soundtrack to **The Last Emperor**.

ryuichi sakamoto

His musical influences and interests are diverse and his style might at any time incorporate elements from electronic music, contemporary classical music, jazz, world music and Japanese pop. Sakamoto has worked with several international directors on a collection of astonishingly diverse productions. After his beginnings with Nagisa Oshima (**Merry Christmas, Mr Lawrence**, 1982) he went on to write scores for a trio of films directed by Bernardo Bertolucci (**The Last Emperor**, 1987; **The Sheltering Sky**, 1990; **Little Buddha**, 1993). The hugely popular and contemporary Spanish director Pedro Almodóvar's film **High Heels** (1991), was also scored by Sakamoto. Unusually for a film music composer, he has also acted in several of the films mentioned above.

interview

I started playing piano when I was three in kindergarten. By the time I was 11 no one was doing it except me. My piano teacher advised me to take lessons in composition. Initially my parents and even myself were against the idea but my piano teacher was very passionate that I should get a musical education so I thought, "Maybe I have something". Although I loved music and played the piano for three hours every day I also liked many different things: science, literature, art, sports, girls, everything. It was only very recently, even a year after we formed the Yellow Magic Orchestra, that I thought, "This is my job for life". When we were working on that first album of YMO, which was '79 to '80, the tracks were influenced by movies, especially Godard movies. Most of my writing has some kind of visual image either realistically or virtually – even when writing pop music I have various images in my head.

My first soundtrack was for **Merry Christmas, Mr**

(1–4) **Merry Christmas, Mr Lawrence**: (2, 4) Sakamoto played the character of Captain Yonoi in the film: "When I saw the rough cut I was shocked by my bad acting, so I put my passion into writing the score to compensate." (2) Bernardo Bertolucci later would ask Sakamoto to write the music for his film **The Last Emperor**, having heard the music for **Merry Christmas, Mr Lawrence**: "He had seen the film and thought that the love scene at the end was the strongest love scene ever in film history. Because that was between David Bowie and myself, two men!"

1

2

3

4

Merry Christmas, Mr Lawrence: "When I wrote the music for this film I was 100 per cent amateur – I didn't know how to write film music! I asked the producer to give me a reference point for writing the film music and his answer was **Citizen Kane**, which, of course, was done by Bernard Herrmann. I knew his music from before, so maybe there was some influence from him. I also wanted to express the complicated relationships through leitmotifs, as they were created enough in the film or by the images, so I had to express that."

Lawrence. I never dreamed I would work on movies although I loved film music a lot – Maurice Jarre was one of my heroes. I was 100 per cent amateur. At our first meeting, Nagisa Oshima, the director, showed me the script and asked me if I wanted to act in the film. Immediately I asked him if I could do the music, as a kind of trade. The story is about a kind of communication and mis-communication between East and West. It's also about love. I worked hard to get the right music that would make us feel a kind of nostalgia, not for a real place, or country or time but a nostalgia for nowhere. I wanted to write music that would sound sometimes oriental for Western people and for Eastern people – something in the middle. I wanted to be in-between.

I wrote the score at the beginning of sampling in the early '80s. The main instrument was the EMU1. I laid out everything with synthesizers and sampling machines and I overdubbed later with piano and some real strings. Back in university, of course, I wrote some orchestral and symphonic pieces but I hated it. I wanted to get away from writing. Synthesizers, computers, samplers were what I was using at the time. At first I didn't know how to proceed so I made a list of cues where I wanted to put the music. I showed my list to Mr Oshima and he said that 99 per cent was the same as he got. So after that everything was done by me.

I wanted to reconstruct the whole story with my music using the Wagnerian idea of leitmotifs. The complicated relationships needed the support of the music to be expressed successfully. This would not have occurred simply by means of images alone. For the scenes in England the music had to be very pure. The young brother represents a kind of human purity and David Bowie ruins this purity and feels guilt and remorse. So as a contrast to this the music had to be pure.

Bertolucci said he loved the film and the music. In fact he said that the love scene at the end of **Merry Christmas, Mr Lawrence** was the most beautiful love scene in the history of cinema. However, when I came to compose the music for **The Last Emperor**, Bertolucci didn't want me to use samplers and synthesizers – he wanted me to write a score and record a real orchestra.

When I first met Bertolucci and we began talking about **The Last Emperor**, I was expecting him to ask me to write the music but once again I was asked to act. I was surprised. I said yes immediately. I spent two months in China and then in Cinecittà in Rome and that was it for the acting part. Then a few months later I got a call from Bertolucci: "Start writing now. We only have two weeks." "What?" I cancelled everything and went back to Tokyo. I had to find some good Chinese instrumentalists in Tokyo and at the same time I had to write some themes. I wasn't so familiar with Chinese music. In fact I rather disliked it. It's close to Japanese music but different also. However, I went to a record shop and bought a 22-record anthology. I listened to everything.

Bertolucci and I had got on well during the shooting but it was completely different in the recording studio. On the first day he arrived at the studio and started to yell, "Where is the big

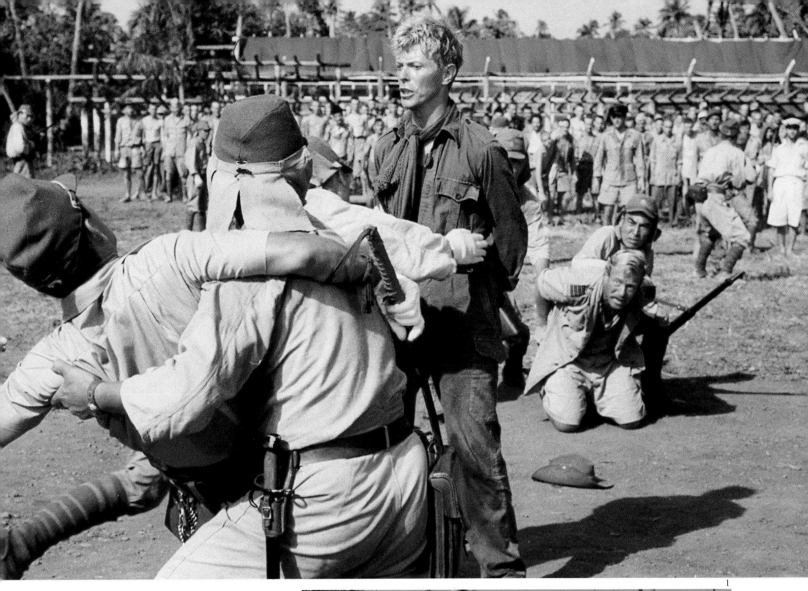

(1–2) **Merry Christmas, Mr Lawrence**: "You know, although it looks like a war film between Japanese soldiers and British soldiers, to me it was a love story, a twisted love story."

film music

(1–6) **The Sheltering Sky**: "There was a special moment for me during this film. When I was writing the music I was watching the video of the film. The camera was very slowly moving towards these two people, so slowly that you could hardly notice. Suddenly I got a view of what the director was seeing in his eyes. I got the feeling that I could share the same aspect." (4) "At the right moment you see the white hat and you hear a moment of the theme music; a simple melody, but it contains mixed emotions – now and the future and maybe the past – the differences of cultures between New York and Africa."

3

4

6

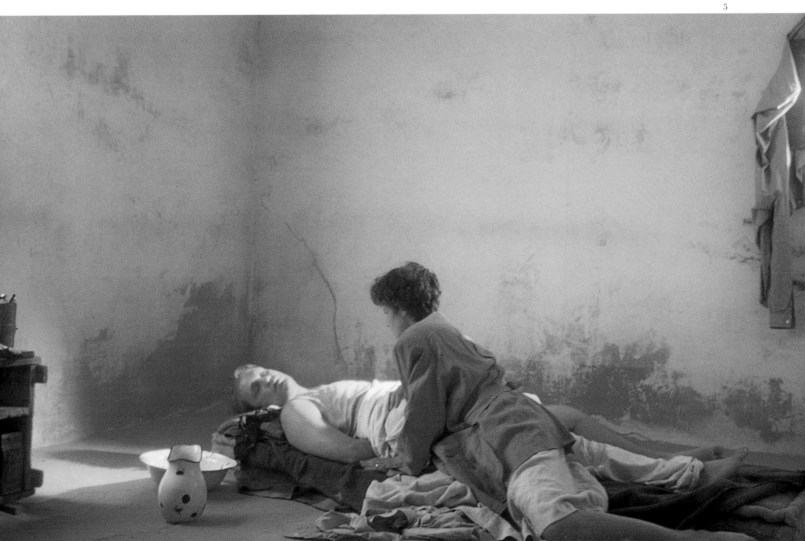

screen?" He only knew the old style of recording film music in front of a big screen, where you look at it and the conductor holds a clock. My method was all computerised. Everything was sequenced even though we used acoustic instruments and an orchestra. Everything was played to the calculated time sequences. Bertolucci didn't understand all this. He didn't have any idea about overdubbing. Scenes would have strings with brass and woodwind to be added later. Bertolucci would shout, "More emotion, Ryuichi, we need brass here! Where is the brass?" I would say, "Bernardo, don't worry, we'll have the brass tomorrow". "No, no, that's impossible!" Gradually, as he observed the process, he began to understand and our communication got better.

The Sheltering Sky also began with a phone call from Bertolucci. He had been in the deep Sahara for six months and he didn't have any idea about what was going on in the world. The Berlin Wall had come down and he was a communist in the '60s, very political. He felt so empty. He had spent all his emotions shooting in the Sahara. He couldn't give me any directions about the music. I did have some opinions and ideas but I wasn't sure. So we listened to lots of music for two weeks. Finally we found Verdi's 'Requiem' and I got him to dub it on to some of the film. Then I left that behind and started to write from scratch.

It took me three or four days to get the first idea of the theme. I tried everything I had at the time – it was so hard to get the right note, the right key. The movie opens with some pre-existing jazz taken from the '20s. It was chosen by Bertolucci.

I liked the idea as it made the contrast between America and Morocco when the people come from New York to the Sahara. Then there's some Arabic chant on the ship. Then, at the right moment, you see the white hat and you hear, very thin, the theme music. It's a simple melody but it contains mixed emotions and mixed times: the present and the future, as well as mixed localities and cultures. There's a tragic feeling because the couple know about their future, how they will end up because they are coming from New York to Africa without any goal. They are travellers without a destination.

I was fanatical about ethnic music at university, I wanted to become an ethnomusicologist, but it's different working with real musicians. Luckily we had a great specialist, Richard Horowitz, who was working on the Arabic music and he knew this music very deeply. This time I used a full orchestra, no samplers. Although I was working in a very Western classical style Bertolucci wanted me to bring up my Japanese-ness in a deeper level, some kind of mystical thing about space and time. I'm not sure I have that 100 per cent. I don't think I'm a typical Japanese person.

Another phone call. This time from Pedro Almodóvar. He wanted me to visit Madrid, introduce me to the city, his friends, and of course to his film **High Heels**. He didn't say why he wanted me for the movie but he did give me one reference which was Miles Davis. He explained how deeply Miles understood Spanish culture. He wanted me to dig into it in the same way Miles had. I even wrote the opening music for the movie but he didn't use my music, instead he used

1

2

3

(1–3) **High Heels**: The only reference given to Sakamoto by director, Pedro Almodóvar, was the sound of Miles Davis: "He explained how deeply Miles understood Spanish culture." In the end Almodóvar was to replace the opening theme with Miles Davis' music: "This often happens with film composition – you write 40 pieces of music and the director will maybe only use half or two thirds. But it's their film, not mine."

1

(1–3) **Little Buddha**: The film charts two concomitant journeys: that of a young Lama monk to Seattle and the spiritual journey of Siddharta to become the Buddha. From his unique musical background, Sakamoto produced a score which was highly successful in expressing this meeting between East and West. (right) Ryuichi Sakamoto conducting his opera 'Life'.

2

3

Miles' music for the introduction. I still don't know how much he liked my music!

Many times I've attended the premiere of a film and let's say I wrote 40 cues, 40 pieces of music, and the director might have used half, and many are missing. I get really frustrated because they even put the music in a different place. But it's their film, not mine. What I have to do is deliver music and hand it to the director or producer. After that they have the freedom to do whatever they want. They can burn it, ruin it, reverse it, place it wrongly, as they like. Of course the composer understands music perfectly, more than anyone, but that doesn't mean that he necessarily has the right point of view about the balance between images and music or even story and music.

Not many directors, in my experience, know music. They don't know how to describe what they want musically. In general it's very hard to express music in words. I have to guess what they want, what they are hearing in their mind. I feel like I'm an interpreter between two languages.

glossary

TERMINOLOGY

Arranging: Close to orchestration. Often involves adapting a musical piece or idea to another context e.g. from piano to orchestra.

Click track: Beats produced digitally at a selected tempo and heard through headphones by players and conductor with the intention of achieving total precision timing.

Counterpoint: The layering of individual melodic lines to create a musical piece.

Cue sheets: Listing of where in the action the music makes its entrances and exits with times and frames.

Dubbing: The moment of truth for the composer. The point at which each cue fits (hopefully) into its alloted place in the film, and is balanced with the other sound elements (dialogue, sound effects etc.).

Emulators: One of the first samplers (made by American company EMU systems), a device that can record sounds and reproduce them across the keyboard. You could have a scale of dogs barking or you could realistically simulate a section of violins.

Glissando: An Italian formation from the French word *glisser*, (to slide). It applies to the effect deliberately achieved by dragging the fingers across the keys of the piano/strings/keys of the instrument.

Ground bass: Popular in 16th- and 17th-century music. A short bass line repeated over and over again with harmonic variations and, if required, a vocal line written above.

Leitmotif/motif: A melody or theme used to denote a particular character, place or even state of mind, a device that derives from 19th-century opera.

Main title: Music over opening credits consisting of the main theme and other leitmotifs acting as signatures for certain characters.

Mickey-mousing: When the music mimics the physical nature of the action, as opposed to playing against the action of the scene. It is so-called because this is a characteristic extremely common to cartoon music, and is therefore often considered out of place in a film where the emotions of a scene are more commonly explored in the music.

Mixing: Once the music has been recorded adjustments can be made to the balance of sound. Certain instruments or groupings of instruments are alloted separate tracks whose dynamics can be enhanced or diminished. Similarly, individual tracks can be "treated" by the use of effects such as delay or graphic equalisation.

Moviola: Before computers the moviola was used for getting pre-scoring timings and assembling the tracks for the dubbing session. The picture was run on the machine and the timings required were taken from a counter. To assemble the recorded tracks the music editor would return to the moviola to cut the music to run in synch with the picture.

Music editor: Oversees the synchronisation of music to film by keeping cue sheets which contain detailed descriptions of the scenes requiring music.

Orchestration: Scoring for an orchestra or instrumental ensemble which, unless clearly defined, can involve artistic decisions concerning instrumentation and dynamics. For this reason many composers prefer to do their own orchestration rather than give their work to a professional orchestrator, or at least give very detailed sketches.

Reel: A film is normally composed of five reels, each approximately twenty minutes long.

Rhythmic cells: Short patterns of

rhythm that can be repeated or used as the basis for variations. A method much favoured by contemporary minimalist composers but pioneered in film by Bernard Herrmann.

Scoring session: Occasion where the music for the film is recorded, frequently in the presence of the producer and director. It may be decided that some cues need to be adjusted by adding or deleting certain beats or sometimes completely rewritten on the spot.

Source music: Music that is an integral part of the scenario e.g. a car stereo, supermarket muzak, nightclub ambience.

Spotting session: Meeting with the director to decide where music is needed. Often the music editor will assist in noting the specific frame where music should be. There will also be creative discussions between composer and director as to the nature of the music.

Streamers: Old method of synchronising the recording of music to film. A diagonal line running from left to right is created by literally scraping the emulsion off the film. The line is equivalent to a determined time e.g. two seconds of film. The composer/conductor must keep an eye on both orchestra and screen to determine the "synch point", the moment when the streamer ends, which is indicated by a burst of light created by making a hole in the film.

Temp track: Pre-existing music that is used as a temporary soundtrack in order to aid the pace of editing and, so it is believed, to give the composer the "feel" of what the director wants from a score.

Vision MIDI: A computer software music-composing system (made by American company Opcode Systems). There are three other similar systems (Emagic Logic, Steinberg Cubase, and Mark Of The Unicorn Performer) around which most film music composers' computer composing systems are based.

INSTRUMENTS

Balalaika: A Russian stringed instrument of the guitar type. It is triangular in shape, has three strings and four movable frets, and is played with a plectrum.

Canvas: A type of electronic sound module replicating many musical instruments.

Celeste: A keyboard instrument from the 1880s in which tuned metal bars are struck by hammers similar to those of the piano.

EMU 1: The first emulator (see above).

Gamelan: Indonesian orchestra consisting of percussion instruments of the fixed-note type, such as xylophones.

Kurzweil: An electronic instrument company originally famed for their synthesizers which realistically simulated the acoustic piano.

Ondes Martenot: Invented by Maurice Martenot in 1928. Electronic instrument similar to the theremin but operated by means of a dummy keyboard thus enabling greater control of pitch.

Serpent: Obsolete brass instrument apparently invented in the late-16th century. It consisted of an S-shaped wooden tube of wide bore, about seven feet long and bound with leather. It was played with a cup mouthpiece and had six finger holes.

Tabla: An Indian drum.

Theremin: Invented by Leon Theremin (Russia) 1927. Early electronic instrument which produces a "pure" sound achieved by the manual operation of an oscillating valve circuit.

picture credits

Courtesy of The Kobal Collection: p 10 **L'Arrivée d'un train à la Ciotat**, Lumière brothers; p 10 **The Battleship Potemkin**, Goskino; p 10 **October**, Sovkino; p 10 **Napoléon**, Societé General De Films/Gaumont/MGM; p 11 **King Kong**, RKO; p 11 **Alexander Nevsky**, SMOSFILM; p 11 **High Noon**, United Artists; p 13 **Psycho**, Paramount; p 14 **East of Eden**, Warner Bros.; p 14 **Forbidden Planet**, MGM; p 15 **Close Encounters of the Third Kind**, Columbia/Tri-Star; p 15 **Jurassic Park: The Lost World**, Universal and Amblin; p 15 **American Beauty**, TN and Dreamworks LLC, photography by Lorey Sebastian; p 15 **The Talented Mr Ripley**, Paramount/Miramax, photography by Phil Bray; p 16 **2001: A Space Odyssey**, MGM; p 17 **Titanic**, 20th Century Fox/Paramount; p 18 **Psycho**, Paramount; p 19 portrait of Bernard Herrmann; p 21 **Citizen Kane**, RKO (1–4); p 21 **The Magnificent Ambersons**, RKO (5–6); p 22 **Beneath the 12-Mile Reef**, 20th Century Fox (1); p 22 **The Day the Earth Stood Still**, 20th Century Fox (2); p 22 **Journey to the Centre of the Earth**, 20th Century Fox (3); p 22 **Jason and the Argonauts**, Columbia (4); p 23 **The Wrong Man**, Warner Bros. (5); p 23 **Cape Fear**, Universal (6–7); p 23 **The Devil and Daniel Webster**, RKO (8); p 24 **Carrie**, United Artists (1); **Psycho**, Paramount (2–5); p 26 **North by Northwest**, MGM (1–6); p 28 **The Bride Wore Black**, Films du Carosse/Artistes Associes (1–4); **Fahrenheit 451**, Anglo Enterprises/Vineyard (2–3, 5); p 30 **Taxi Driver**, Columbia/Tri-Star (1–5); p 31 Bernard Herrmann conducting; p 32 **The Age of Innocence**, Columbia, photography by Phillip Caruso; pp 34–5 **The Man With the Golden Arm**, United Artists (1–5); p 37 **The Ten Commandments**, Paramount (4–5); p 41 **Cape Fear** (1962), Universal (1); p 41 **Cape Fear** (1991), Universal (2); p 42 **The Age of Innocence**, Columbia, photography by Phillip Caruso; p 43 portrait of Maurice Jarre; pp 46–7 **Lawrence of Arabia**, Columbia (2–5); p 49 **Doctor Zhivago**, MGM (1–3); p 50 **Doctor Zhivago**, MGM (1–3); pp 52–3 **Witness**, Paramount (1–6); p 54 **Dead Poets Society**, Touchstone (2); pp 56–7 **Fatal Attraction**, Paramount (1–3); p 57 portrait of Maurice Jarre; p 58 **Basic Instinct**, Carolco; p 60 **Planet of the Apes**, 20th Century Fox (2, 4–5); p 63 **Chinatown**, Paramount (1–3); pp 64–5 **Alien**, 20th Century Fox (1–6); pp 66–7 **Poltergeist**, MGM/United Artists (1, 3–6); p 68 **Basic Instinct**, Carolco (1–3); p 70 **Midnight Cowboy**, United Artists; p 72 **Goldfinger**, United Artists (1, 4); p 74 **Midnight Cowboy**, United Artists (2–4); p 77 **Midnight Cowboy**, United Artists (1); p 78 **Out of Africa**, Universal (1–3); p 80 **Out of Africa**, Universal (2); p 82 **Sudden Impact**, Warner Bros.; p 86 **The Cincinnati Kid**, MGM/Filmways (4); p 87 **The Cincinnati Kid**, MGM Filmways (5); p 89 **Tango**, Argentine Sono (1–3); p 92 **Dirty Harry**, Warner Bros. (2); p 94 **The Piano**, Jan Chapman Productions/CIBY 2000; p 96 **The Cook, the Thief, His Wife and Her Lover**, Allarts/Erato (2–3); p 99 **The Hairdresser's Husband**, Lambert/TFI/Investimage (3–4); p 100 **Drowning by Numbers**, Allarts (2); **The Piano**, Jan Chapman Productions/CIBY 2000 (2); p 103 **The Piano**, Jan Chapman Productions/CIBY 2000 (4); p 104 **Gattaca**, Columbia (2); p 105 **Gattaca**, Columbia (6); p 108 **Betty Blue**, Constellation-Cargo/Alive-Gaumont Productions; pp 110–11 **Betty Blue**, Constellation-Cargo/Alive-Gaumont Productions (1, 3–4); p 113 **Vincent & Theo**, Belbo/Central/Telepool (3–4); p 115 **Vincent & Theo**, Belbo/Central/Telepool (7–8); p 117 **The English Patient**, Tigermoth/Miramax (1); p 117 **The English Patient**, Tigermoth/Miramax (1); p 117 **The English Patient**, Tigermoth/Miramax, photography by Phil Bray (2); p 123 **Mishima**, Warner Bros. (8); p 124 **Kundun**, Touchstone/Capra/De Fina, photography by Mario Tursi (1); p 24 **Kundun**, Touchstone/Capra/De Fina (2–3); pp 126–7 **Powaqqatsi**, Cannon (1–6); p 127 **Koyaanisqatsi**, The Institute for Regional Education (8); p 129 **The Truman Show**, Paramount, photography by Melinda Gordon (1–2); p 129 **The Truman Show**, Paramount (3–4); p 134 **Dead Ringers**, 20th Century Fox (1, 3); p 134 **The Fly**, 20th Century Fox (7); p 136 **Naked Lunch**, Recorded Picture Co./1st Independent (1); p 137 **Naked Lunch**, Recorded Picture Co./1st Independent (7); p 144 **eXistenZ**, Alliance Atlantis, photography by Avo V. Gerlitz (1–2); p 146 **Edward Scissorhands**, 20th Century Fox; p 148 **Beetlejuice**, Geffen/Warner Bros. (3–4); pp 150–1 **Batman**, Warner Bros. (1–5); p 153 **Batman**, Warner Bros. (3); **Edward Scissorhands**, 20th Century Fox (1–2, 5); pp 154–5 **Edward Scissorhands**, 20th Century Fox, photography by Zade Rosenthal (4, 6); p 157 **The Nightmare Before Christmas**, Touchstone/Burton/Dinovi (1–2); p 158 **Mars Attacks!**, Warner Bros., photography by Bruce Talamon (1–3), p 160 **Three Colours: Red**, MK2/CED/France 3/CAB Productions/Tor Productions/Canal +; p 162 **The Double Life of Véronique**, Sideral/Tor Studios/Canal + (1, 3); p 164 **Damage**, Skreba/Nef/Channel 4/Canal + (2); p 165 **Damage**, Skreba/Nef/Channel 4/Canal +, photography by Sophie Baker (4); p 166 **A Short Film about Love**, Film Polski (1); p 167 **A Short Film about Killing**, Film Polski, photography by Pathé Releasing Ltd. (9); p 169 **The Secret Garden**, AM Zoetrope/Warner Bros. (2–6); p 170 **Three Colours: White**, MK2/France 3/CAB Productions/Tor Productions/Canal + (1–4); p 171 **Three Colours: Blue**, MK2/CED/France 3/CAB productions/Tor Productions/Canal+ (5–6); p 172 **Three Colours: Blue**, MK2/CED/France 3/CAB Productions/Tor Productions/Canal + (3); p 174 **The Sheltering Sky**, Warner Bros.; pp 176–7 **Merry Christmas, Mr Lawrence**, Recorded Picture Company-Cineventure-Asahi/Oshima (1–2); pp 180–1 **The Sheltering Sky**, Warner Bros. (3, 5–6); p 183 **High Heels**, El Deseo S.A./CIBY 2000 (1, 3); p 184 **Little Buddha**, CIBY 2000/Recorded Picture Co., photography by Laurie Sparham (1); p 184 **Little Buddha**, CIBY 2000/Recorded Picture Co., photography by Richard Blanshard (2); p 184 **Little Buddha**, CIBY 2000/Recorded Picture Co., photography by Angelo Novi (3).

Courtesy of the Ronald Grant Archive: p 2 **Lawrence of Arabia**, Columbia/Tri-Star; p 6 **The Silence of the Lambs**, Orion, photography by Ken Regan; p 8 **King Kong**, RKO; p 11 **Symphony of Six Million**, RKO; p 12 **Gone With the Wind**, Turner Entertainment; p 14 **The Graduate**, Embassy; p 14 **Star Wars**, Fox Lucas Film; p 27 **Vertigo**, Paramount (7–8); p 36 **The Ten Commandments**, Paramount (3); p 37 **The Magnificent Seven**, United Artists (1); p 41 **Cape Fear**, Universal (3); p 44 **Dead Poets Society**, Touchstone Pictures, photography by Francois Duhamel; p 46 **Lawrence of Arabia**, Columbia (1); p 54 **Dead Poets Society**, Touchstone Pictures (1, 3); p 59 portrait of Jerry Goldmith; p 60 **Planet of the Apes**, 20th Century Fox (1, 3); p 66 Jerry Goldsmith conducting (2); p 72 **Dr. No**, United Artists (3); p 72 **Goldfinger**, United Artists (5); p 73 **Diamonds are Forever**, EON-United Artists (7); p 77 **Midnight Cowboy**, United Artists (2–3); p 80 **Out of Africa**, Universal (1); p 84 **Hell in the Pacific**, Selmur Pictures (2–3); p 86 **Rollercoaster**, Universal (1); p 86 **Strangers on a Train**, Warner Bros. (2); p 87 **The Cincinnati Kid**, MGM/Filmways (6–7); pp 90–1 **Bullitt**, Warner Bros. (1–2, 4); p 92 **Dirty Harry**, Warner Bros. (1, 3); pp 98–9 **The Hairdresser's Husband**, Lambert/TF1/Investimage (1–2, 5); p 101 **Drowning by Numbers**, Allarts (1); pp 102–3 **The Piano**, Jan Chapman Productions/CIBY 2000 (1, 3, 7); pp 104–5 **Gattaca**, Columbia (1, 5, 7); p 106 **The Draughtsman's Contract**, BFI/United Artists (3–4); p 111 **Betty Blue**, Constellation-Cargo/Alive-Gaumont Productions (5); pp 114–5 **Vincent & Theo**, Belbo/Central/Telepool (1, 5); p 120 **Mishima**, Warner Bros.; p 121 Philip Glass; p 122 **Mishima**, Warner Bros. (1); p 127 **Koyaanisqatsi**, The Institute for Regional Education (7); p 130 **Dracula**, Universal (1–4); p 132 **The Silence of the Lambs**, Orion; p 134 **Dead Ringers**, 20th Century Fox (2); p 134 **The Fly**, 20th Century Fox (5–6); p136 **Naked Lunch**, Recorded Picture Company/1st Independent (3–5, 8); pp 138–9 **The Silence of the Lambs**, Orion (1–6); p 141 **Ed Wood**, Touchstone (1–4); p 142 **Ed Wood**, Touchstone (1); p 148 **Beetlejuice**, Geffen/Warner Bros. (1–2); p 162 **The Double Life of Véronique**, Sideral/Tor Studies/Canal +; p 164 **Damage**, Skreba/Nef/Channel 4/Canal + (3); p 165 **Damage**, Skreba/Nef/Channel 4/Canal +, photography by Sophie Baker (5); p 165 **Damage**, Skreba/Nef/Channel 4/Canal + (6); p 166 **A Short Film about Love**, Film Polski (2–5); p 167 **A Short Film about Killing**, Film Polski (6–8); p 171 **Three Colours: Blue**, MK2/CED/France 3/CAB/Tor Productions/Canal + (7–8); p 172 **Three Colours: Red**, MK2/CED/France 3/ CAB/Tor Productions/Canal + (1–2, 4); p 176 **Merry Christmas, Mr Lawrence**, Recorded Picture Company-Cineventure-Asahi/Oshima (2); pp 180–1 **The Sheltering Sky**, Warner Bros. (1–2, 4); p 183 **High Heels**, El Deseo S.A./CIBY 2000 (2).

Courtesy of Hulton Getty Picture Library: p 7 Portrait of John Barry, photography by H. V. Drees; p 72 John Barry with the moviola (2); p 80 John Barry.

Courtesy of Pic Photos: p 73 John Barry (6).

Courtesy of The Bridgeman Art Library: p 113 'Bedroom at Arles' (1888) by Vincent Van Gogh, Rijksmuseum, Amsterdam/The Bridgeman Art Library (5); p 114 'Sunflowers' (1887) by Vincent Van Gogh, The Metropolitan Museum of Art, New York/The Bridgeman Art Library (2); p 115 'Starry Night' (1888) by Vincent Van Gogh, Musée D'Orsay, Paris/The Bridgeman Art Library (6).

Courtesy of BFI Films: p 74 John Barry (1).

Courtesy of Christian Him's Jazz Index: p 83 Lalo Schifrin; p 84 Lalo Schifrin (1).

Courtesy of the Lebrecht Collection: p 95 Michael Nyman, photography by Mary Robert; p 101 Michael Nyman, photography by Mary Robert (3); p 106 Michael Nyman, photography by Jim Four (2).

Screengrabs: p 118 **The English Patient**, with thanks and acknowledgement to Tigermoth/Miramax (1–2); pp 122–3 **Mishima**, with thanks and acknowledgement to Warner Bros. (2–7, 9–10).

Visual material contributed by Elmer Bernstein: p 33 Portrait of Elmer Bernstein; p 36 pages from score for **The Ten Commandments** (1–2), with thanks and acknowledgement to Paramount; p 39 pages from score for **The Magnificent Seven** (2–3), with thanks and acknowledgement to United Artists.

Visual material contributed by Lalo Schifrin: p 86 Page from score for **The Cincinnati Kid** (3), with thanks and acknowledgement to MGM/Filmways; p 91 page from score for **Bullitt** (3) with thanks and acknowledgement to Warner Bros.; p 93 portrait of Lalo Schifrin and Dizzy Gillespie.

Visual material contributed by Michael Nyman: p 96 Page from score for **The Cook, the Thief, His Wife and Her Lover** (1), published by Michael Nyman Ltd./Chester Music Ltd., with thanks and acknowledgement to Allarts/Erato; p 103 pages from score for **The Piano** (5–6), published by Michael Nyman Ltd./Chester Music Ltd., with thanks and acknowledgement to Jan Chapman Productions/CIBY 2000; p 104 pages from score for **Gattaca** (3–4), published by Michael Nyman Ltd./Columbia Pictures Industries; p 106 page from score for **The Draughtsman's Contract** (1), published by Michael Nyman Ltd./Chester Music Ltd., with thanks and acknowledgement to United Artists.

Visual material contributed by Gabriel Yared: p 109 Portrait of Gabriel Yared; p 110 **Betty Blue** (2), with thanks and acknowledgement to Constellation-Cargo/Alive-Gaumont Productions; p 113 **Vincent & Theo** (1–2), © 1990 Virgin Music Ltd., with thanks and acknowledgement to Belbo/Central/Telepool; **Vincent & Theo**, with thanks and acknowledgement to Belbo/Central/Telepool (3–4); p 117 portrait of Gabriel Yared, photography by Terry Loft (3); p 118 page from score for **The English Patient** (3), © 1996 Tiger Mother Music, with thanks and acknowledgement to Tigermoth/Miramax.

Visual material contributed by Howard Shore: p 5 Page from score for **The Silence of the Lambs**, composed by Howard Shore (ASCAP), published by Orion Pictures Corporation © 1990 All Rights Reserved; p 133 portrait of Howard Shore; p 134 page from score for **The Fly** (4), composed by Howard Shore (ASCAP), published by Brookfilms Ltd. © 1986 All Rights Reserved; p 137 pages from score for **Naked Lunch**, composed by Howard Shore (ASCAP), published by Halemount Ltd./Recorded Picture Company © 1991 All Rights Reserved (5–6); p 139 page from score for **The Silence of the Lambs**, composed by Howard Shore (ASCAP), published by Orion Pictures Corporation © 1990 All Rights Reserved (7); pp 142–3 pages from score for **Ed Wood**, composed by Howard Shore (ASCAP), published by Touchstone Pictures Music and Songs Inc. © 1994 All Rights Reserved (2–7); p 145 Recording sessions.

Visual material contributed by Danny Elfman: p 147 Portrait of Danny Elfman, photography by L. M. Jones, 1998; p 152 pages from score for **Batman** (1–2), composed by Danny Elfman, with thanks and acknowledgement to Warner Bros.; pp 152–3 **Edward Scissorhands** (4–6), composed by Danny Elfman, with thanks and acknowledgement to 20th Century Fox.

Visual material contributed by Zbigniew Preisner: p 161 Portrait of Zbigniew Preisner, photography by Anna Wloch; p 164 portrait of Zbigniew Preisner (1); p 169 portrait of Zbigniew Preisner (1); p 173 portrait of Zbigniew Preisner.

Visual Material contributed by Ryuichi Sakamoto: p 175 Portrait of Ryuichi Sakamoto; p 185 Ryuichi Sakamoto conducting his opera 'Life'.

index